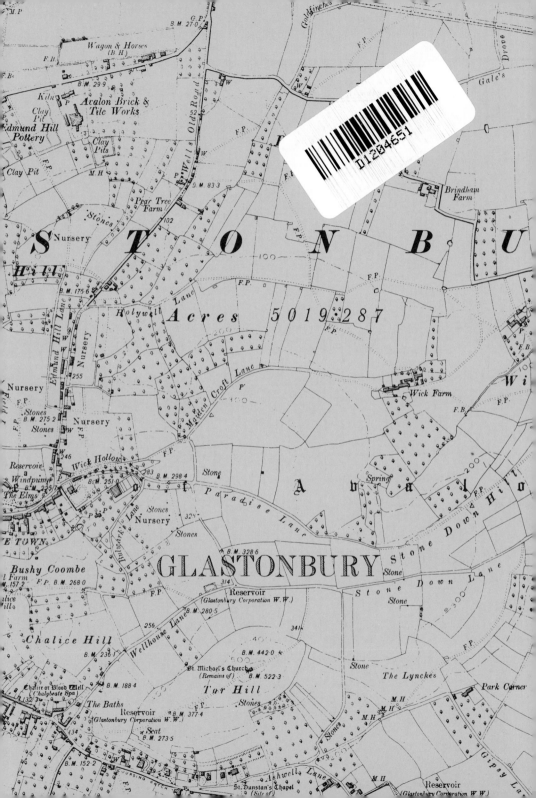

NEW LIGHT
on the
ANCIENT MYSTERY
of
GLASTONBURY

NEW LIGHT
on the
ANCIENT MYSTERY
of
GLASTONBURY

John Michell

Glastonbury, Somerset

First published in 1990 by
GOTHIC IMAGE PUBLICATIONS
7, High Street, Glastonbury, Somerset BA6 9DP

Cover illustration by John Michell
Original photographs by S.Bostock

Designed and set in 11/12pt. Monotype Bembo
by Creative Technology Associates, Somerton, Somerset
Imagesetting by LP&TS, Aller, Somerset
Printed by Castle Cary Press, Somerset

British Library Cataloguing in Publication Data
Michell, John *1933-*
    New Light on the Ancient Mystery of Glastonbury
    1. Somerset, Glastonbury
    I. Title
    942.383
    ISBN 0-906362-14-8
    ISBN 0-906362-15-6 pbk.

Dedication & Acknowledgements

In memory of two Glastonbury authors,
Anthony Roberts, to whom this book is specially dedicated,
and Gino Schiraldi

Special thanks to those who have contributed to this book, especially Frances Howard-Gordon who guided and edited it; to her and Jamie George who commissioned it, encouraged it at every stage and published it; to Richard Elen for his expertise and personal involvement in its production; to Simant Bostock for his lovely photographs of the Avalonian landscape; to Christine Rhone for advice and help and the photograph on page 8; and to Olivia Temple for the photograph on page 33.

TABLE
of
CONTENTS

Introduction

The spiritual priority of Glastonbury—the 'holiest earth of England'—
an image of paradise—landscape and legends—a sanctuary from time
immemorial—the privileged Twelve Hides—their sacred light—the
spirit of Celtic culture—Tudor sacrilege—the modern renaissance.

PART I: PREHISTORIC TIMES

1. The Primordial Paradise

A landscape wheel—the Glastonbury archipelago—the wandering
tribes—their community of purpose—their economy—their feasts—
their estates—their culture—spiritual perception—stars, myths and
landscape—tribal sanctuaries—sacred isles.

2. The Seven Island Stars
of Arthur the Great Bear

The seven chartered isles—Avalon and the wooden church—Beckery's
Irish pilgrims—St. Brigit's chapel—King Arthur in the Chapel Perilous—his mystical experience—the legend of Godney—St Guthlac at
Marchey—Meare and St Benignus—his miracles—the vines of Panborough island—Nyland hill—the seven island chapels—correspondence
with the Great Bear—the island planisphere—the Great Bear, Arcturus
and King Arthur—traditions of the seven-star constellation—the stellar
landscape in old China—Glastonbury Tor the pole star—the planetary
Round Table—the Maltwood zodiac—its conception—'marks of authenticity'—simulacra—a powerful image—antiquity of the seven-
island constellation.

3. The Somerset Elysium

The Fortunate Isles—Glastonbury as Avalon—as universal pole—as an Elysium—Arthur in the underworld—Gwynn ap Nudd and his realm below the Tor—St Collen dispels his enchantment—the Hollow Tor—the abduction of Guinevere—initiation—the primeval golden age—the Grail quest.

4. Megalithic Magic in the Age of Giants

The tribes form settlements—the first Glastonbury farmers—the exit from paradise—hunters, miners and traders—priests and megalithic builders—their contact with the underworld—their use of light—megalithic alignments—Irish mounds—the powers of the earth—the invocation of giants—the exploitation of thought-forms—Chinese geomancy—the manipulation of earth forces—the age of Taurus—Mother Nature's giant progeny—the Titans—agricultural deities—Saturnus and Kronos—memories of the golden age—Glastonbury and the Blessed Isles.

5. The Gigantic Mysteries of Glastonbury Tor

The labyrinth on the Tor—Geoffrey Russell's discovery—a work from the age of giants—the St Michael line—Burrowbridge Mump—Avebury—Silbury hill—a landscape of ritual—the Mump and the Cheesewring—the serpents and the straight line—a pilgrimage path—poetic images—the linear chant—a legend of the line—a symbol of sacred union on the Tor.

6. The Giant-Killers

Phantom monsters—the raising of elementals—Stonehenge and Merlin—the landing of Brutus—Corineus the giant-killer—the downfall of the giants—the rise of Apollo—Arthur at Brent Knoll—early Celtic Britain—magical warfare—Druid spells—the power of Excalibur.

7. Arthur the Sun-King and the Zodiacal Round Table

The dawn of Aries—the Bronze age—its splendour—Celtic craftsman-ship—solar orientations—the solar civilization and its law—the rule of the twelve gods—twelve-tribe nations—their cycle of festivals—their music and myth—the zodiacal order—King Arthur in the Glastonbury landscape—the Twelve Hides and the twelve-part mythic cycle—Arthur in other lands—the Order of the Round Table—Arthur's Chariot—the clock of the Great Bear—reading the Glastonbury land-scape—its twelve divisions—image of the Heavenly Jerusalem—the zodiac and the Round Table—the transformations of Arthur—the constancy of his mission—the twelve revivalists—Arthur's vigil.

8. Life and Religion in the Kingdom of Arthur

Glastonbury's priestly rulers—the local economy—rights and obliga-tions—a relic of the Celtic system—the twelve-tribe society—its bene-fits and limitations—its reflection of the zodiac—the science of enchant-ment—the breaking of the spell—the rise of commerce—Glastonbury's wealth—"the Bristol of its day"—the Druidic social order—its decline and suppression—new cults at the dawn of Pisces—the reformation of Druidry—the Christian revelation.

PART II: THE CHRISTIAN REVELATION

9. The Glastonbury Legend

The coming of St Joseph of Arimathea—denigrators of the legend—sceptics and partisans—mystical clergymen—royal visitors to Avalon—the flowering thorn—Jesus in Britain—Cornish legends—the 'Secret of the Lord'—the Celtic mysteries—their influences on Christianity—the Priddy legend—a divine foundation—the priority of Albion—the Virgin at Glastonbury—galloping gullibility—its possible function—a key to the mysteries.

10. Joseph of Arimathea
and the Ancient Wooden Hut

11. Twelve Saints and the
Mysterious Conversion of the Celts

12. The Wattle Church and the Hall of Light

The focus of the mysteries—the wooden hut shrine in China, Japan, Rome, England—the Roman Regia—the Chinese Ming T'ang—its primitive character—simplicity of its rituals—its sacred dimensions—the Ming T'ang and Stonehenge—the Stonehenge orientations—Glastonbury's wooden hut—the foundation ritual—a heavenly sanctuary and the invocation of Paradise on earth.

13. The Foundation Pattern

Summarized history of the Old Church—its unaltered condition—the rebuilding after the fire—the new St Mary chapel—joined to the main church—St David's pillar—its inscribed plate—text of the inscription—the pillar rediscovered—the pyramid in the Abbey cemetery—the finding of King Arthur's bones—their identification—the trepanned skull—the burial site rediscovered—Bligh Bond's excavation—the Masonic tradition—the octagonal site plan—the position of St Joseph's church—the symbolism of proportions and measures—the development of the foundation pattern.

14. The Glastonbury Revelations

F. Bligh Bond appointed to the Abbey ruins—his qualifications and interests—his mystical views—psychic archaeology—*The Gate of Remembrance*—automatic writing—Johannes the monk—his tales of the old days—Bond's understanding of spiritualism—his disgrace, exile and death—his influence in the Glastonbury revival—an English Bayreuth—the Glastonbury ritual revived—the magical order of W.B. Yeats—his spirit medium consulted by Bond—*The Gospel of Philip the Deacon*—a spate of mystical booklets—Bond warned against spiritism—his poetic guidance—his achievement and its limitations.

15. The Stonehenge Prototype and the Meaning of the Foundation Pattern

The pattern on the paving—William of Malmesbury's account—its effect on Bligh Bond—an astrological site plan—the advent of 'Brother Simon'—*The Company of Avalon*—the spirit of Romualdus—his description of the foundation pattern—another account—further details from an American medium—gematria and sacred architecture—Bligh Bond's revelations—the foundation plan disclosed—its application to Stonehenge—Bond's misconception over the site of St Joseph's church—his quest for the founders' cells—the octagonal pattern—the twelve cells positioned—the tomb of St Joseph—Bond's search for the Grail chalice—the Philosopher's Stone at Glastonbury—the Glastonbury legend for pilgrims—the mystic treasure—alchemical transmutation—contemplation of meaning—towards the centre of the mystery—knowledge and faith—the light of prophecy.   *page 145*

16. Glastonbury in the Light of Prophecies

John Leland at Glastonbury—astonished by its library—the ancient chronicle of Melkin the Bard—Melkin's prophecy of Glastonbury—Carley's translation and comments—Islamic features to the prophecy—its alchemical flavour—St Joseph and the Grail—the Great Work—the mystic tomb—the *linea bifurcata*—the zodiac on the church floor—a hidden relic—concealment of Abbey treasures—the theme of an earthly paradise—its implication in the foundation pattern—the science of initiation—an invitation to paradise—the paradisial archetype—its image as a city—Blake and Plato—the limitations of civilization—the ready-made pattern—its relation to the Grail—its invocation in ancient Glastonbury—its accessibility today.   *page 161*

Bibliography

page 169

Index

page 173

LIST
of
ILLUSTRATIONS

The Twelve Hides of Glastonbury, according to Warner in 1826. This area represents the territory ruled by Glastonbury's Abbot in the Middle Ages, when the sanctuary area far exceeded the original 1440 acres.

Introduction:
The Glastonbury Mystery

There are many mysteries at Glastonbury, but they are all rooted in one great mystery: how is it that this small place, isolated among the Somerset marshes, plays such a leading part in the spiritual history of Britain? Other religious centres, Canterbury, Westminster, Winchester, have had their periods of glory, but the fame of Glastonbury is unique and has endured longer than that of any other English sanctuary. In medieval Christendom the site of the first English church, at the west end of Glastonbury Abbey, was called the 'holiest earth of England', and its precincts were sanctified as a model of earthly paradise, where the souls of the dead found their easiest passage to heaven.

This reputation did not begin with Christianity but evidently derived from very early times indeed. The evidence of this is in Glastonbury's landscape and the remarkable legends which have settled upon it. Moreover, from time immemorial Glastonbury and the lands around it enjoyed special privileges in law, appropriate to a most venerable sanctuary. As in the case of Delphi, where a federal assembly of twelve tribes upheld the rights of Apollo in his sacred territories, the area known as the Twelve Hides of Glaston was subject only to divine law and was administered by priestly rulers. No king, judge or bishop from beyond the Twelve Hides had any authority there. These rights were confirmed in successive charters by British, Saxon, and Norman kings, including the pagan Caedwalla, king of Wessex in the seventh century. Every king attempted to 'entrench' these rights, binding his successors to them for all times to come.

The traditional origin of Glastonbury's privileges is that a pagan ruler,

King Arviragus in the first century A.D., bestowed twelve hides or 1440 acres of land upon twelve early Christian missionaries, led by St. Joseph of Arimathea.

Like many traditions of the early Church, this probably reflected an earlier foundation legend from the time when Glastonbury was a Druid sanctuary. No traces have been found of any buildings from that period, but the great prehistoric earthwork, known as Ponter's Ball, which runs across high ground about two miles east of Glastonbury, is thought to have marked one of the boundaries of the sacred precinct. It is likely, therefore, that Glastonbury's special status as a heavenly sanctuary, beyond the ordinary laws of the land, was acknowledged long before the introduction of Christianity.

Behind all the religious history of Glastonbury lies the real reason for the special character of the place. The sanctity of Glastonbury is not a matter of human convention, nor did it arise from any historical event. It was decreed directly by nature. That conclusion is made obvious to anyone who visits Glastonbury, especially at dawn or evening when the mystical quality of the light over its landscape is particularly intense. As one enters the Glastonbury landscape, over the hills which surround its lowlands, one's perception of natural light and colour subtly changes. Around the towering cone of Glastonbury Tor is a countryside which gives the impression of being somehow different from any other. It can seem wistful, nostalgic, other-worldly, even intimidating, but it is never quite ordinary.

Those who recognize the spirit of the Celtic culture can find it there, in the limpid greenery of its hills and meadows and secluded among its moorland tracks and waterways, edged with willows and summer garlands of honeysuckle and wild roses. Seeing this, one ceases to wonder why the place has been compared to paradise, why so many mystics and holy men throughout history have been drawn to it and why its medieval abbey was able to boast the finest collection of saintly bones and relics in England.

When Henry VIII in 1539 laid sacrilegious hands upon Glastonbury Abbey and its Twelve Hides, hanged its abbot on the Tor, sent his dismembered body for piecemeal exhibition about the country, violated the sanctuary and turned it to profane use, he broke a long-lasting religious tradition which had survived all England's enemies and invaders. Yet he was as powerless as King Canute over the forces of nature, and those forces, as we have seen, were the cause of Glastonbury's sanctity in the first place. They are still as ever active. Though Glastonbury is no longer an important centre of priestly religion, the spirit which first made it so is constantly urging towards a renaissance. History marks out Glastonbury as the place where the forms of every new religion and way of thought are first manifested in England. New forms and thoughts are discernible there today. There are hints of old prophecies being fulfilled, of ancient mysteries revealed, as the Piscean Age gives way to Aquarius. For those who are interested in such things, in the spiritual reality behind the material facade of history, the mystery of Glastonbury is of high topical interest. It is examined in the following chapters, which outline the development of Glastonbury's magical legend and thus restore the chain of sacred tradition which links the ancient past to the present and extends into the future.

PART I:
PREHISTORIC GLASTONBURY

Glastonbury Tor and the Isle of Avalon in winter floods

Chapter One
The Primordial Paradise

Glastonbury Tor forms the hub of a great landscape wheel, extending in every direction as far from its summit as the eye can see. This is a wide area, for the Tor is visible from the Black Mountains of Wales to the north-west and from the hill of South Cadbury in the opposite direction, a total distance of about 70 miles. A circle of 30 miles in diameter would approximately contain the region which lies beneath the visual dominance of Glastonbury Tor.

About 12,000 years ago, when the Ice Age glaciers receded, allowing the repopulation of southern England, the Tor and its foothills were almost entirely insulated by an inlet of the sea from the Bristol Channel. The sea was studded with island hills, and across this watery landscape ranged the earliest tribesfolk, navigating between their islands in canoes and coracles.

In every way, physically and mentally, these people were born exactly the same as we are today. Their way of life is therefore of constant interest, for it shows how the free human spirit, conditioned only by its native environment, tends naturally to express itself.

Anthropologists who have made the acquaintance of nomadic tribespeople in different parts of the world are often impressed by the sense of fulfilment in their lives. In general, they have no chiefs, laws or judges, and there is very little dissension among them. They enjoy long discussions which are joined in by people of all ages. Everything is done according to custom and by general agreement. This state was referred to by Plato in the *Laws* as the ideal society, preceding the artificial state of civilization. There are no possessions or permanent marriages, and children belong to the community as a whole rather than to individual parents. Linked together by common needs and purposes, the people are so united that it is as if they share together their eyes, ears and limbs.

A description of tribal life, as it would have been experienced by the earliest people of Glastonbury, is given by Richard Muir in *Celtic Landscapes*. The early tribes "migrated around an eternal circuit, harvesting each resource which the changing seasons provided. There were salmon in the rivers, eggs to be gathered on the sea cliffs, fish, seals and stranded whales along the coast and limpets on the rocks, while the rich woodlands harboured wild cattle, deer and horses, fungi, fruit, roots and shoots... Yet we should not imagine for an instant that the communities were composed of aimless, ineffectual savages. To live well under the Mesolithic economy one needed to have an intense awareness and understanding of Nature, know the habits and behaviour of the intended prey and when each edible plant would release its fruits and where it could be found."

With few artificial aids, the early tribes existed almost entirely by their culture, which was based on intimate knowledge of their native countryside. They lived, one might say, in the style of aristocrats, owning in common a broad acreage, made up of many different and varied estates, each of which they visited at the appropriate season. The people around Glastonbury Tor were particularly favoured, for their estates included woods and meadows, sea coasts, marshes and islands, a territory which could provide all the best things to eat in every season for those who knew how to gather them.

The knowledge and disciplines needed to maintain this way of life were not simply, or even primarily, material. Like all uncivilized people everywhere the people of the Glastonbury estates inhabited a world of spirit. The perception of those who spend their lives in close observation of nature transcends the material aspect of things and penetrates to the spiritual realm which underlies it. Thus it is seen that each kind of plant and animal has its own genius which, if properly approached and propitiated, will multiply its kind and provide abundance. The shrines where the various genii have located themselves are each visited in the course of a year, and so the tribal journey has the character of a constant

An ancient sanctuary: the knoll at Compton Dundon with its church and venerable yew tree.

pilgrimage from station to station across an adventurous, haunted landscape, whose every feature has its own spirit and its associated legend, song, customary ritual and day of the year.

The nomad tribespeople were spellbound throughout their lives by a myth which they acted out in the course of their travels. It was an astronomical and geomantic myth about the wanderings of the seven planets and the wheeling of the constellations around the celestial pole. The adventures of the stellar gods and heroes were transferred to earth and became attached to certain spots about the country. Thus the order of the heavens was mirrored in a symbolic landscape where hills corresponded to stars and provided earthly locations for episodes in stellar mythology.

In those early days were established the traditional sacred places of the countryside. Every notable rock, mound, hollow, tree, pond, spring, river bend and convergence of streams or trackways contributed its legend to a year-long epic which described the interactions of the heavenly gods and the spirits of the local landscape. The myth which led the Glastonbury tribes around the sacred places of their landscape was surely the prototype of Glastonbury's Arthurian cycle.

It is still possible to identify some of the aboriginal shrines in the countryside around Glastonbury Tor. The clues are rarely archaeological for, apart from their delicately shaped little flint knives and arrowheads (the 'fairy bolts' of later folklore), the only evidence of the tribal camp sites are the bones and shells from an endless round of feasts. The old sacred places are mostly reliably discerned by the human eye and sensibility, which are the same today as they were thousands of years ago. Those who know the countryside around Glastonbury will recognize certain spots whose aspect and traditions proclaim their ancient sanctity. Examples include Wookey Hole and the cave sanctuaries of Cheddar; the village green at Priddy on the Mendip hills above, with its legend that Christ once walked there; the site of Wells Cathedral beside gushing springs of water, famous for curing aches; the springhead at Doulting, dedicated to St Aldhelm, where the river Sheppey has its source; the rock above a stream where now stands Pilton church, also with a legend of a visit by Jesus, and the grassy mound bearing the church at Compton Dundon and its ancient yew tree.

Tribal sanctuaries were also located on islands in the seas and marshes below the Tor. They are now green hills rising out of the Somerset levels. Many of them, as at Meare, Burtle, Godney, Nyland, Brent Knoll, Martinsea and Beckery, retained their sanctity into Christian times and became the sites of churches or chapels. One of these former islands, the lovely hill at Panborough, seems in its name to commemorate the old nature god, whose presence is still hinted at by the wreaths of ivy hanging from its trees. On its sides grapes were once cultivated, and in the Middle Ages it was the chief vineyard of Glastonbury Abbey.

The isle of Godney, or 'God's Island', where the ancient chapel, rebuilt, is now the parish church.

Chapter Two
The Seven Island Stars
of Arthur the Great Bear

Seven of the islands within Glastonbury's Twelve Hides were of special significance and were held sacred from the earliest times. They are repeatedly and exclusively named in the old Glastonbury charters by which a succession of English kings confirmed the absolute supremacy of the Abbot of Glastonbury within his realm.

These seven islands had a privileged status which exempted them from the ordinary laws of the land. Their traditional freedom from taxation was confirmed in the Domesday Book, and no officials from outside the Twelve Hides, not even the monarch himself, had any rights over them. Their names, as listed together with Glastonbury in the tenth-century charter of King Edgar, are: "Bekaria quae parva Hibernia dicitur, Godeneia, Marteneseia, Ferramere, Padenaberga, et Andredeseia."

On each of the seven chartered islands in medieval times stood an ancient chapel. Their histories are sparsely recorded, but examination of their legends, and especially of their topographical relations, provides an important clue to the understanding of Glastonbury's mystical landscape.

The following, with the modern spelling of their names, are the seven island sanctuaries of Avalon.

1. The Isle of Avalon, the site of Britain's first Christian foundation. Its wooden church, said to have been built by Joseph of Arimathea, was probably the model for the chapels on the other six islands.

2. Beckery, also known as **Little Ireland**. From the early days of Glastonbury Abbey it was much visited by Irish pilgrims, for in the fifth century this small, low island was inhabited by St Brigit, who followed St Patrick to Glastonbury. She dwelt beside an old oratory dedicated to St Mary Magdalene, and her relics, including a prayer bell and her spindle, were displayed in a pilgrims' chapel on the island. In his chronicles of about 1400 John of Glastonbury mentioned a hole in the southern wall of the chapel. Pilgrims used to crawl through it in order to obtain forgiveness of their sins.

St Brigit's chapel was under the direct protection of Glastonbury's abbot, and there is a record of it being "sumptuously restored" in the thirteenth century, together with the chapel at Godney. By the eighteenth century it was a ruin. There is now no visible evidence of its site, but excavations at the end of the nineteenth century, and again in 1968, uncovered the foundations of two successive chapels, the earliest of Celtic or Saxon origins. Also found was evidence of prehistoric settlement or encampments.

The history of Beckery is closely interwoven with that of Glastonbury and the other sacred islands. John of Glastonbury identified it as the site of the Chapel Perilous referred to in the Arthurian romances. He tells how King Arthur, while resting in the convent of St Peter on Wearyall Hill, was ordered through a dream to visit the Beckery chapel at dawn. A servant who preceded him there and stole a golden candlestick from the altar was struck dead for sacrilege. When Arthur approached the chapel he found it guarded by two flashing swords, but after he had said prayers he was allowed to enter. In the chapel an aged hermit was performing Mass, assisted by none other than the Virgin Mary. She offered up her infant son as a sacrifice for the world, and she presented King Arthur with a crystal cross which became one of the treasures of the Abbey. After this experience Arthur adopted a new coat of arms, green with a silver cross and an image of the Virgin with her child, and dedicated his life to the service of God.

3. Godney or 'God's island', where the former chapel was replaced in 1839 by a simple church to the Holy Trinity on the same site. Traces of the old building remain in the Norman west front, and in the windows

The Arms of King Arthur, adopted after his mystical experience in the Beckery chapel, were assumed by Glastonbury Abbey.

On the west side of the ruined tower on Glastonbury Tor, the figure of a woman milking a cow is traditionally identified as St. Brigit, who was once a milkmaid. In the fifth century she dwelt on one of Glastonbury's sacred islands, Beckery (meaning 'little Ireland' in the Irish language), and her relics attracted many Irish pilgrims to the Abbey.

are some curious medieval fragments of stained glass, with figures of ducks and mermaids. The sanctity of this lonely spot is illustrated in its ancient legend, discreetly given in Latin in Warner's *History of Glastonbury*, that the great flocks of birds which found sanctuary on and around Godney island always respected the chapel and would never foul its roof.

Near Godney at the end of the first millenium B.C. was built the famous lake village, a collection of circular, thatched huts on a platform raised above the shallow waters and connected to dry land by wooden causeways.

4. Martinsea or **Marchey**, a slight rise in the flat, watery landscape, where there was formerly a chapel dedicated either to St Martin or St Guthlac. Marchey shares its name with another sacred island, March in the Cambridgeshire fens, and in that same district is also found the legend of St Guthlac. He became a hermit on a desolate isle in the marshes, Crowland near Peterborough, and there he fought off demons with a whip. A similar legend was probably attached to Marchey. Its origins are certainly pre-Christian.

11

5. Ferramere is an early name of **Meare**, the village at the eastern end of a former island which includes Westhay. Just off its northern shore lay an Iron Age lake village, similar to that near Godney. The special sanctity of Meare was acknowledged in the fifth century, when its ancient chapel was dignified by the tomb of another famous Irish saint claimed by Glastonbury, Benignus or Beonna. He was a disciple of St Patrick and succeeded him as Glastonbury's second Abbot. Like St Brigit's chapel at Beckery and the burial place of St Patrick in the wooden church at Glastonbury, St Benignus's shrine at Meare received many pilgrims from Ireland.

According to his legend, St Benignus was a worker of miracles, even after his death. At Meare he struck water from the ground with his staff which, when planted, took root and grew into a large tree. In the eleventh century it was decided to bring the relics of St Benignus to Glastonbury Abbey for reburial before the high altar. While they were being translated from Meare, a series of miracles occurred. A column of light streamed down upon the Meare chapel and a rainbow canopy appeared over Glastonbury Abbey. As the boat carrying the saint's bones moved along the river to Glastonbury, many cures took place among the onlookers and there was further healing of the sick at a religious service held near the point of landing. On that spot, where probably stood a chapel or shrine marking one of the boundaries within the Twelve Hides, was built the church of St Benignus, now called St Benedict's. It was placed and orientated in line with Glastonbury Abbey, on the westward extension of the Abbey's axis.

In the fourteenth century the present church at Meare was built, probably on the site of the former chapel. Within it, on the south side of the chancel arch, are the arms of Joseph of Arimathea. The fine old house adjoining the church was once a residence and courthouse of Glastonbury's abbots.

6. Panborough, the former vineyard island, is one of the loveliest of Avalon's sacred hills. Somewhere upon it was a chapel, thought to have been dedicated to St Padan, who is also the patron saint of Nailsea church some sixteen miles to the north.

7. Andrewsea or **Nyland** is a majestic island hill, rising out of Cheddar Moor near the northern extremity of the Twelve Hides. On three sides it is surrounded by a cove of hills, but to the south the view opens up, revealing the entire Vale of Avalon with its green islands, backed by Glastonbury Tor. Nyland is the natural gateway to this enchanted landscape.

The former chapel on Nyland Hill has vanished without trace. It was probably dedicated to St Andrew, but it may have been the St Guthlac's chapel alternatively situated at Martinsea. The parish of Nyland lay outside the main borders of the Twelve Hides but shared in their privileges. One of the duties of the Abbot of Glastonbury's waterman in the thirteenth century was to navigate the Abbey barge on ceremonial visits to Andrewsea and the other sacred islands.

In Celtic times these islands were inhabited by hermits. One of these, dwelling on the island of Andrewsea, who died while on a visit to his fellow hermit at Beckery, is mentioned in the story of Arthur's initiation at the Chapel Perilous. In the days of Glastonbury Abbey the island chapels were maintained and served by the monks. Why these particular seven islands were so distinguished has long been a mystery, for several of them are far less outstanding in size and height than other, unfamed island hills in the same district. The answer emerges when the seven islands are plotted together on a map. They form a pattern which closely approximates to the pattern of the seven stars in the Great Bear constellation. Glastonbury corresponds to the star Dubhe on which the constellation pivots.

The constant veneration by the Glastonbury monks of these seven islands suggests that they knew the secret of their symbolic arrangement. If, as F. Bligh Bond affirmed in *The Company of Avalon*, that there was an Abbey geomancer, such knowledge would have been within his province. It is clear from their traditions, however, that the sanctity of the seven islands was recognized before Christian times. The first people who saw their likeness to the Great Bear would have been those whose eyes were trained to observe nature's symbolism, and that implies that the early tribes of Glastonbury, who journeyed in their imaginations across a stellar landscape, were the first to detect in their watery realm

The little islet of Martinsea or Marchey is the most secluded of Glastonbury's seven sacred islands. Its medieval farmhouse, now in ruins, probably adjoined the long-vanished chapel.

Two of the former sacred islands are now green hills: the majestic Nyland (above) and Barrows Hill at Panborough.

those particular seven islands which reproduce the Great Bear.

The relevance of this constellation of island sanctuaries to the history and mythology of Glastonbury is immediately apparent. From very early times the Great Bear has been associated with King Arthur. Welsh scholars derive Arthur's name from 'Arth Fawr', the Great Bear, and he is also associated with Arcturus, the brightest star in the northern hemisphere, whose position in the sky is indicated by the last two stars in the tail of the Great Bear. Arcturus in Greek means the Keeper of the Bear. In Spanish it is named Arturo or Arthur, and old English writers (such as John of Trevisa in 1389) made plain its traditional connection with Arthur by calling it Arthurus.

In *Star-Names and their Meaning* R.H. Allen quotes an earlier authority, W.H. Smyth, on the Arthurian symbolism of the Great Bear.

> "King Arthur… typified the Great Bear; as his name— Arth, bear and Uthyr, wonderful—implies in the Welsh language; and the constellation, visibly describing a circle in the North Polar regions of the sky, may possibly have been the true origin of the Son of Pendragon's famous Round Table."

The early English, writes Allen, called the Great Bear the home of King Arthur. It was also called Arthur's Wain or Wagon, being seen as the vehicle in which Arthur circled the pole. Another name for the Great Bear is the Plough. By that name it is again associated with Arthur as *Arator*, the Ploughman. As such he is depicted in the ancient Welsh story of Kulhwch and Olwen, where Arthur is an agriculturalist and ploughs down a vast hill. Those names, however, are not so old as the bear symbol, which was applied to the seven-star constellation long before carriages and ploughs were invented. The bear-name is remarkably universal. It is recorded in astronomical traditions from Asia to northern Europe, and the early settlers in North America were surprised to find that many tribes of Indians referred to the Bear constellation. Also from the Indians came its modern American name, the Big Dipper.

The Wain and the Plough are farmers' names but the Bear is from the language of hunters. In many stellar myths, Arcturus and the other stars

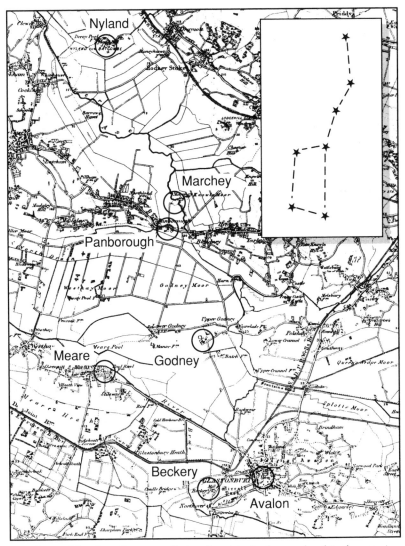

The figure of the Great Bear constellation (inset) is closely reproduced in the grouping of the seven sacred islands of Avalon.

of its constellation, Boötes, are represented as a huntsman following his hounds (the stars known as Canes Venatici) in pursuit of the Great Bear. In prehistoric times bears were plentiful in England; they lived on in the wild until about the eighth century A.D. Thus one can imagine in outline the form of myth which accompanied the journeys of the early tribes between the seven islands of Glastonbury's Great Bear. Arthur was the spirit guardian of those islands, the keeper of the Bear and also the leader of the bear hunt. His legendary adventures were ritually enacted as the tribes moved around the central pole of their territory, imitating the revolutions of the Great Bear around the pole star. Their totem was the bear; the image of their chief god was Arcturus and the Great Bear constellation, and the title assumed by their leader was Arth Fawr or Arthur.

According to the foundation legend of Chinese geomancy, the first man to observe the correspondence between the stars in the sky and the natural features of the landscape was the first ruler, Fu Hsi. "Looking upwards he contemplated the images in the heavens; looking downwards he discerned the patterns on earth." Thus the earliest form of Chinese geomancy was based on the perception of a stellar landscape. From that early perception developed the elaborate system of geomancy which produced the civilized landscape of China. In the days of tribal nomadism, however, things were simpler. Every tribal territory was seen as a celestial planisphere, a great wheel on which were imprinted the constellations visible in the sky above.

The similarity between the group of seven sacred islands and the stars of the Great Bear suggests that other constellations were recognized in the Glastonbury landscape. Their forms and positions would only have been approximately accurate in relation to the actual stars, for the landscape planisphere was a symbol rather than a precise chart of the heavens. It seems plain, however, that Glastonbury Tor represented the pole star, which is the star nearest to the imaginary line through the firmament produced by the northward extension of the earth's axis. Because of the earth's wobble on its axis, the celestial pole describes a near-circle among the stars over a period, by traditional reckoning, of 25,920 years. At the centre of its wanderings is the constellation of Draco, the Dragon, and thence may have derived the name of Arthur's father, Pendragon, the Dragon's Head. The earliest image of the Tor would therefore have been the head of a guardian dragon, watching over the treasures of Avalon and protecting with its coils the symbolic world-centre in imitation of Draco encircling the celestial pole.

The Great Bear formation of the seven islands of Glastonbury supports the intuitions of several previous writers who have suggested that in ancient times the Glastonbury landscape was marked with some form of celestial design. Early Welsh chronicles associate Arthur's Round Table with the Great Bear and hint at its former location on earth, while the following enigmatic statement occurs in the medieval romance, *La Queste del Saint Graal*.

> "The Round Table was constructed, not without great significance, upon the advice of Merlin. By its name the Round Table is meant to signify the round world and round canopy of the planets and the elements in the firmament, where are to be seen the stars and many other things."

This passage caught the attention of Katherine Maltwood, who in the summer of 1929 was staying near Glastonbury, illustrating an edition of the *High History of the Holy Graal*. She suspected that the episodes in the Grail Quest were located in the district, and as she looked at maps her eye was caught by certain configurations in hills, boundaries and waterways which resembled symbolic figures. A lion and a woman, outlined in part by the sinuous river Cary near Somerton, were the first figures she noticed. She took them as symbols of Leo and Virgo, and completed her zodiac by recognizing ten other landscape effigies in a circle ten miles in diameter with its centre near Butleigh, three miles south of Glastonbury Tor. This circle to her mind was Arthur's original Round Table.

Katherine Maltwood's book, *A Guide to Glastonbury's Temple of the Stars*, and her other writings on the same theme, have had a considerable influence on modern perceptions of Glastonbury.

She was one of the few in her time who understood that the ancients did indeed create symbolic, astrological landscapes, and though many have scoffed at her ideas, others have seen a profound truth behind them. Her most prestigious reviewer, the esoteric writer, René Guénon, discerned "marks of authenticity" in the astrological features of the Maltwood zodiac, and concluded that her thesis "can not easily be set aside as purely fantastic." He was particularly impressed by Maltwood's surmise that the secret of the zodiac had been passed on by the Druids to the monks of Glastonbury, and had also been guarded by the Knights Templar, the reputed keepers of the Grail.

Katherine Maltwood believed that the Glastonbury zodiac was fashioned, through amendments and additions to natural features, by a foreign people, perhaps the Sumerians who might thus have given their name to Somerset, about 5,000 years ago. That idea is by no means impossible, and anthropologists recognize that tribal people are inclined to see symbolic shapes in the folds of hills and rivers. The weak point in Maltwood's vision was her literal expression of it. Many of her effigies seem random and ill-defined and best classified as 'simulacra', examples of the tendency in nature and the human eye, working together, to create apparent symbols and living forms in clouds, rocks and landscapes. Yet through those effigies she created a powerful image, infectious to the imagination, and effective in awakening twentieth-century perception of the large-scale, geomantic works of the ancients.

The Maltwood zodiac, however one evaluates it, has nothing at all to do with the seven Glastonbury islands which form the Great Bear. As shown in later chapters, a solar zodiac was at one time laid out across the Glastonbury countryside, but that also had no real similarities to Katherine Maltwood's effigy system. The stellar landscape long preceded any zodiacal scheme. There can be no certainty about the date when the seven Glastonbury islands were first seen as the Great Bear and acquired their Arthurian associations, but the slender clue, that Arthur was sired by Pendragon, suggests that it was at a time when the pole star was located in the head of Draco, about 12,000 years ago, at the very end of the last ice age.

Chapter Three
The Somerset Elysium

Somerset is the Summer Land, so named in reference to that ideal realm of Celtic mythology, a land of perpetual youth where it is always summer and trees and plants yield their fruits all the year round. That land is no longer to be found on earth, but visions of it are commonly described in British folklore. Like St John's New Jerusalem, it appears as an island floating in the sky, mostly to the west in the mists at sunset. Celtic fishermen see it as an archipelago and have named it the Fortunate Islands and the Islands of the Blessed. It was known as the place where the souls of the dead first proceeded on their journey to the other world.

The island hill of Glastonbury, outstanding among its group of smaller islands, is appropriately identified with Avalon, another name for that insular realm which gives access to paradise. Avalon means Isle of Apples, and the name is well suited to Glastonbury because of the ancient apple orchards which still flourish on the lower slopes of its hills. Nature has endowed Glastonbury with all the traditional features of Avalon, its springs, groves, gardens, vineyards and green upland meadows. The Seven Island Stars of Arthur the Great Bear and Glastonbury's seven charted islands correspond to the seven Islands of the Blessed. At Glastonbury, therefore, are all the components of an Elysium, a central sanctuary perceived as a reflection of heaven on earth and made complete by a feature with all the attributes of Mount Meru, the symbolic pole of the universe. That feature, of course, is Glastonbury Tor.

The early tribespeople moved in a roughly circular orbit across the face of their country, following the revolutions of the stars around the pole of the heavens. Every nation, consisting of tribes with a common language and culture, recognized a national sanctuary which was regarded as the *omphalos* symbolizing the celestial pole of the ecliptic and forming the centre of the whole world. Typically it was a high mountain with its summit reaching up to heaven and with caverns in its interior leading down into the the underworld. The area around it was dedicated to the gods and was preserved as an Elysium. An annual convention was held there, usually at midsummer, when all the tribes of the nation came together for festival and ceremony, to renew old acquaintance and to discuss matters of common interest. It was also the tribal necropolis, sanctified by the relics of heroes and forefathers.

Archaeologists have shown that Glastonbury was a prehistoric burial place, and its former character as an Elysium is further proclaimed by its physical appearance, the names which have been applied to it and its earliest legends. The physical indication is quite unmistakable: even at first sight Glastonbury Tor stands out as the dominant feature of its district and a natural symbol of the world-centre mountain. This is supported by its name. It is possible that the first syllable in 'Glastonbury' derives from an old British word for oak or woad, and it has also been linked with the name of Glasteing, a legendary early settler at Glastonbury mentioned by William of Monmouth; but there is no reason to doubt the obvious explanation, that it is a simple translation from Glastonbury's former Celtic name, Iniswitrin, Isle of Glass or Crystal Isle. A glassy isle is mythologically a place of enchantment. Within it is Caer Wydr, the Glass Castle, and Caer Siddi, the Fairy Fort, also translated as the Spiral Castle. The country where these places are to be found is Annwn, the Celtic land of Faery. In *The Spoils of Annwn*, a poem attributed to the sixth-century Welsh bard, Taliesin, is described how Arthur sailed there to rob its ruler of his magical, pearl-rimmed cauldron which gave sustenance to all who were worthy of it. This vessel seems to have been an early version of the Holy Grail, and Arthur's quest for it in Annwn foreshadows the location in Christian times of the Grail Quest at Glastonbury.

Other items of Welsh bardic history tell of various encounters between Arthur and the lord of the underworld whose name in some

A view from Barrows Hill, Panborough, over the 'Moors Adventurous' towards Glastonbury Tor.

accounts is Gwynn ap Nudd. Many such old tales were retold in Christian romances of the Holy Grail and were incorporated in the Lives of semi-mythical saints, popular in the Middle Ages. In one of these, the anonymous *Life of St Collen*, the realm of Gwynn ap Nudd is anchored to the geography of this world, having its entry at Glastonbury Tor.

The story of St Collen is that, after an adventurous life in the service of religion, he found a quiet hermitage at Glastonbury under a rock below the Tor. This was probably in the lovely little valley between the Tor and Chalice Well, where springs of mineral waters burst out from the earth and once formed a rivulet down to the river Brue. There today are the peaceful Chalice Well gardens, and traces have been found of a former community of anchorites, commemorated until recently in the name of a nearby inn, The Anchorage. Their tradition has been maintained by modern mystics, such as the novelist Dion Fortune, whose dwelling opposite the gardens is now occupied by the Arthurian scholar and Glastonbury revivalist, Geoffrey Ashe.

One day St Collen heard two men outside his cell discussing Gwynn ap Nudd. Having spent his life combating pagan beliefs, he disliked this talk and went out to argue with the couple. Gwynn and his faery court, he said, were just old-fashioned demons. The two men stood their ground and informed the saint that he would soon have to explain that to Gwynn himself. Later there came a messenger to Collen's cell, ordering him to confront Gwynn at the top of the Tor by midday. The order was backed up by threats, so Collen took a vessel of holy water and climbed up to the place appointed. There he found a most beautiful castle, surrounded by a court of noble youths with fine horses, lovely women and an orchestra of fairy musicians. Within the castle Gwynn ap Nudd, seated on a golden throne, received him kindly and offered refreshments which Collen, who knew about the enchanting properties of fairy food, refused to take. When Gwynn boasted about his possessions and mentioned the ornamental red and blue costumes of his followers, Collen replied that the colours symbolized the intense heat and cold to be experienced in hell. He then scattered his holy water around, breaking the fairy illusion and causing Gwynn with his castle and court to vanish. In the cold light of Christian reality St Collen found himself alone on the windy Tor.

There are undoubtedly caves and pot-holes below the Tor, but no one in modern times has discovered the way into them. Rumours of a hollow Tor are still heard in Glastonbury and are renewed from time to time by someone's dream or vision. The tradition was active in the sixteenth century, when Elis Gruffudd recorded the belief that King Arthur never died but is sleeping in a cave "under a hill near Glastonbury" (which could either be the Tor or the hill at South Cadbury, one of the reputed sites of Camelot), and that "he appeared and conversed with many people in many strange ways three hundred years ago."

In several of the Arthurian romances the king of the Summer Land is called Melwas. His citadel was Glastonbury Tor in the Isle of Glass. There for a time he imprisoned Arthur's queen, Guinevere, playing the part of Hades in a Celtic version of the story of Persephone's abduction by the lord of the underworld.

These stories were first written down in Christian times and were adapted accordingly. Many of their themes were far earlier, that of

Glastonbury Tor as an entrance to inner earth being probably one of the oldest. An important feature of the archetypal world-centre mountain within an Elysium is its cavern. The earliest shrines were caves, leading down into the realm of the dark Earth Goddess. Therein are the shades and spirits which provide guidance through dreams and oracles, and there too are the nightmare creatures of the abyss which sometimes appear on the surface as spectres and phantom beasts. Corresponding with this subterranean world is the subconscious, intuitive side of the mind which was the side most needed, and therefore most developed, by the wandering tribespeople.

Those of a tribe who were prepared to undergo initiation into nature's secrets and to acquire the insights of a shaman were conducted into a cave to keep vigil in the darkness. There it was contrived that they should experience all the horrors and dismal images which are latent in the imagination, and upon returning to the sunlit world above they were spiritually reborn, having known death and being thus freed from fear in this life and thereafter.

Balancing its subterranean aspect, each tribal Elysium had its upper regions which were dedicated to the celestial powers. The gods of heaven have their natural shrines on mountains and high hilltops, and signs of their presence take the form of luminous visions or lights in the sky, such as sometimes can be seen today over Glastonbury Tor. Iniswitrin, the Crystal Isle of Glastonbury, was thus perfectly adapted as a paradise at the centre of a paradisial country, the Summer Land. As such it was no doubt experienced by the tribes who first roamed that country, living off the fat of the land and assembling each year on their Isle of Avalon. Like people of every age, they had their share of grief, pain, tragedy and bereavement, but overall their lives were a round of feasts and celebrations. Religion, philosophy and politics were all unknown to them. They inhabited a primeval Golden Age, a period of innocence and plenty which has long been lost and can never by any rational process be regained. It is renewed, however, in the instincts of every new-born child, and it haunts the memory of every soul throughout life. Glastonbury has the power of stirring up memories of the golden past, and that is presumably the reason why it has retained and generated such a rich mythology. Tradition and revelation are both active there; it constantly attracts those who are responsive to such things, and the attraction they feel is the same as that which drew the ancient tribes to make it their Elysium, their spiritual home and the central pivot of their migrations.

The Grail Quest is the search for an ancient secret, something which has been lost but was once apparent, and when it was known on earth it created the atmosphere of a golden age. It was said by the Irish mystic, A.E., that the golden age has never departed but that we have lost the ability to see it. The quest, in that case, is partly a matter of perception. Those who follow it have before them the example of the first people at Glastonbury, whose perception allowed them to see it as an island of heavenly enchantment and its Tor as the location of fairyland. The paradise they inhabited was made for them by nature, but they were responsible for maintaining it as such, and this they did in the only way possible, by keeping in harmony with nature's spiritual forces. Mundane life being easy, contact with spirit was almost their full-time occupation. Theirs was the 'primordial vision', said by Guénon to be one of two components of the Grail, the instrument of paradise on earth. The other is the 'primordial tradition', the addition of which makes it possible to obtain that ideal state wherein the comforts and culture of civilization are combined with the spiritual perception of the old tribal wanderers.

Chapter Four
Megalithic Magic in the Age of Giants

The questions of how and why people give up travelling and settle down to agriculture have never been resolved. Every nation has done so at different times, but we still debate whether civilization is a desirable sign of progress, a stage towards the fulfilment of human destiny perhaps, or an aberration, a crime against human nature and a mark of folly and impiety. The old Greek philosophers made no judgment on this, but declared that civilizations had everywhere risen and fallen throughout the ages. At regular intervals they perish through the forces of nature, alternately by fire and flood.

In about 4,000 B.C.—so archaeologists reckon—the pattern of life around Glastonbury suffered a radical change. The sea retreated somewhat from the Somerset levels, leaving areas of swamp and allowing the growth of trees on lands formerly submerged. A new kind of people emerged, farmers. At first they were cautious, scattering seeds over small plots during the tribal journey, and returning later in the year for the harvest. Soon they grew bolder and more ruthless. They cut down trees, enclosed fields and gardens, lived in permanent dwellings and bred herds of cattle and swine.

The old wandering life was over, but it was still reflected in the calendar of fairs and festivals around the country, each marking a certain stage in the hunter's or farmer's year. Many people, such as herdsmen, traders, craftsmen, pilgrims and party-goers, had business at these fairs, and the tradition of travelling was thus to some extent preserved; but the first step towards civilization was a step out of the primeval paradise, and it was irreversible.

With the beginning of agriculture and settlement, the Glastonbury landscape received its first artificial imprints. From about 3,500 B.C., villages of thatched huts were built on the islands of the marshes, and a network of straight, wooden causeways was laid across the waterlogged ground to link them. Stretches of these causeways, up to more than a mile long, are still being discovered below the peat which has overgrown them, and the archaeological evidence which they have provided, together with objects from the island settlements, have given insights into the economy of the early Glastonbury farmers. They appear to have led hearty lives, enjoying the benefits of a developed agriculture and other crafts, and feasting on the local wildlife, which included many types of sea and fresh-water fish and birds such as pelicans, black grouse and sea eagles which are now quite unknown in the district. They mined lead and other metals on the Mendip hills, and by at least the second millenium B.C. they had established trade routes to foreign countries as far as the Mediterranean.

Coeval with the first farmers were the first priests and the first megalith builders. All over Britain, particularly in the western, rocky parts, an early priesthood set up a network of stone circles, monoliths, dolmens and colossal earthworks in connection with a mystical science. Some of the stones they erected are so large and heavy that engineers today are uncertain about the methods which could have been used to move them. Yet more impressive than any single monument is the vastness of the megalithic work as a whole. The system was created over many generations, each contributing much of its labour and resources to completing the task. Finally, by the beginning of the second millenium B.C., the whole of Britain and the western coastlands of Europe were covered with megalithic structures which extended even to remote islands, uninhabited since prehistoric times.

The reasons for undertaking this great work were obviously connected with the practical needs of the early cultivators. When nomadic life gives way to settlement, populations increase and the earth is required to produce more sustenance. The people of the megalith-building societies were concerned above all with the growth of their crops and the fecundity of the animals they reared or hunted. They

From about 4000 B.C. the islands in the Glastonbury lowlands were linked by wooden trackways, laid over the marshy ground. This reconstructed section near Shapwick shows the technique of the work. Its original carved elegance can only be imagined.

needed, therefore, to maintain contact with the underworld, for within the earth were the powers which renewed fertility. Also of the underworld were the oracular spirits of ancestors and the telluric forces which were personified as giants.

It is commonly agreed among archaeologists and prehistorians that the rituals of the megalith builders were directed towards the earth deities and the souls of the dead. Many of their structures consisted of massive, stone-lined chambers, either below the earth's surface or buried within mounds. They may have served as royal tombs or as reliquaries for preserving sacred bones, but generally their apparent purpose was for initiations and other rites.

In addition to their underworld symbolism, megalithic temples, both below and above ground, were designed in relation to light. At stone circles and other places of assembly, the position of the sun or moon on the horizon at the times of the important festivals was marked by stone or earth alignments. The purpose of these was not so much to allow observations of the heavenly bodies as to integrate rays of light and shadows within seasonal ceremonies. With light came astrological influences. A topographical design connected together all megalithic structures in a series of straight alignments, with linked them also with the natural features of the landscape and with the forces of heaven.

This overview, of an integral, country-wide network of ritual magic centres, conveys a certain meaning. It implies that the centres were somehow in communication with each other. Since the prime use of every ancient temple was for invoking spirits, the form of communication between the megalithic ritual centres was presumably spiritual, involving the powers and vital energies of the earth under the influence of cosmic forces. Modern researches at stone circles have recorded electromagnetic and radionic anomalies at their sites, but they have also shown how inscrutably subtle and elaborate was the magical technology of the megalith builders. There is clearly no possibility of understanding their form of science in terms of our own.

The key to megalithic science is to be found in its underground locations. The surface of the earth was the habitation of nature spirits, familiar and placable, but below it was the awesome realm of the goddess and her menagerie of giants and monsters. It was a dangerous undertaking for the ancient priests to invoke the titanic powers of earth, but it could be accomplished by the arts of theurgy, necromancy and commanding spirits. Magicians recognize the importance of performing their operations at certain times and dates, astrologically propitious, and there is ample proof that the priests of the megalithic temples timed their invocations to coincide with certain patterns of light and energy from the heavenly bodies. Martin Brennan in *The Stars and the Stones* has shown that the ancient stone chambers of Ireland, covered with earth mounds and entered by narrow, stone-lined passages, were orientated to receive light from the sun or moon on particular days. The best known is Newgrange, north of Dublin, where the rising midwinter sun casts a beam down the sixty-foot length of the passage to illuminate the inner chamber on the shortest day of the year.

The symbolic meaning of a shaft of light piercing the darkness of an underground chamber is plain enough. No other pair of natural images

The universal legend of how megalithic structures were the work of supernatural forces, commonly personified as giants or dwarfs, is illustrated in this 17th-century Dutch engraving.

could more clearly depict the union of the two eternally opposite principles in creation, typified by light and dark, positive and negative, male and female and their innumerable correspondences. In the ancient world symbolism was always related to function, so there can be no doubt that the symbol of light penetrating darkness within the womb of the earth illustrates a more significant form of union which took place inside the megalithic mound chambers. Alchemists refer to it as the sacred marriage, for it wedded together the two most essentially opposite elements, or aspects of divinity, the receptive powers of earth below and the positively charged, solar and cosmic rays from above.

Performed within the chambered mounds which served as alchemical retorts for the fusion of elements, the sacred marriage had the effect of renewing and revitalizing the fertility of the earth goddess, and the elemental powers within her were then most easily invoked. One of the purposes for which these powers were used is indicated by the traditional explanation of how megalithic structures were raised. Wherever these monuments occur, they are classified in folklore as the work of supernatural beings, usually giants.

The numerous megalithic works popularly attributed to giants include many of the largest stone and earth monuments in Britain. Cornwall, the legendary last refuge of giants in Britain, provides many examples of giants' castles, tables, seats and graves, and the huge granite capstones of Cornish dolmens are still known as quoits because the giants used to play games with them.

Prominent features of the landscape, which are now assumed to be natural, are often included among the reputed fabrications of the giants. The legend is particularly common in the West Country, where it is said that giants piled up the moorland rocks and tors and built the towering cliffs of St Michael's Mount. The Mount's twin rock, Mont St Michel off the coast of Normandy, has a similar legend, for its traditional founder was Gargantua, the giant whose name is associated with mountain sanctuaries across France and Italy. His brother giant at St Michael's Mount was named Cormoran.

In all the giant legends the reference is to elemental forces, the telluric powers which upheave mountains and activate volcanoes. They act spontaneously, beyond human control, and the works attributed to Gargantua, Cormoran and the giant fraternity were certainly created by these natural forces.

It must always have been apparent that megalithic monuments were of human design, yet they are included with tors and mountains among the traditional works of giants. The solution to that paradox may be that both mountains and monuments were raised by the same powers of earth, but in the case of the megaliths those powers were artificially directed. The ancient priests, as we have seen, worked magically through the earth and dared to invoke the titanic forces of the underworld. In the normal processes of magic they would have conjured up thought-forms, like the 'tulpas' of eastern magicians, shaped and adapted to perform the tasks required of them. Having that power, they would inevitably have used the forms they created to assist them in the work of megalith building. Tradition may therefore be right, and megalithic monuments may largely have been erected by giants.

If the giant forces of the earth were harnessed to the work of moving

The Cheesewring, Bodmin Moor

large stone blocks for the construction of megaliths, they might have been used for even greater things. In many parts of the country are found strangely placed or shaped rock formations which geologists suppose to be natural features, simply because of their huge size. The Dartmoor tors and the Cheesewring rock pile on Bodmin Moor are examples of West Country outcrops which appear in some ways artificial, and have often been thought so, but are far too massive to be the work of human hands. They could, however, be creations of the human mind and will, commanding through magic the dark and mighty powers of earth.

The main reason why an ancient priesthood should have wanted to re-shape the natural landscape has to do with geomancy. In the Chinese annals of geomancy (*feng-shui*) it is recorded that in archaic times hills were raised, lowered or given new forms in order to bring them in harmony with an overall landscape composition which both reflected and conditioned the field of sacred energy (*ch'i*) over the countryside. The psychic character and appropriate use of any spot were determined by the quality of its *ch'i*, but this could be changed by the arts of geomancy. At first locally and later on a national scale, the Chinese geomancers strove to domesticate the wild energies of the earth, channelling them in ways which were favourable to human activities, and advising on the most spiritually advantageous sites for tombs, houses and villages.

From rugged, mountainous districts, where the earth's energies well up through cracks and fissures, *ch'i* was conducted to other parts of the country via a series of aligned temples and monuments. These spiritual paths were called dragon lines (*lung mei*). Upon them were placed temples to sanctify the energy as it passed down the land, revitalizing the spirit of each part and thus raising the level of its fertility, prosperity and happiness.

At the same time, the system of spirit sources, aligned with temples, tombs, pagodas and other monuments, gave the priests and geomancers control over their societies, allowing them to spread their influence and gain intelligence.

In many parts of the world, in America, Europe and throughout the East, ancient landscapes are marked with a similar pattern, of precisely aligned monuments, shrines and landmarks, radiating outwards from sacred centres and sometimes linked by paths. The version of this system in Britain is based on megalithic monuments, located on straight alignments, which their discoverer, Alfred Watkins in the 1920s, called leys. These are so closely comparable with the dragon lines of China that a common function is indicated. As has already been pointed out, the function to which the ley system seems best and uniquely adapted is the conveyance of spirit or energy, and that accords with the stated purpose of geomancy in China.

The neolithic priests of Britain, predecessors of the Celtic Druids, are clearly identified by their monuments as geomancers, and they were therefore aware of the sacred energies which the Chinese call *ch'i*. The earth's natural radiations and magnetic currents form part of *ch'i* but do not entirely comprise it, for sacred energy has its metaphysical and aesthetic aspects. Like the subtle energies of the body, and those detected by dowsers in the earth, it can be moved by thought, and it can be diverted and attracted in much the same way as the innocent human spirit can be attracted, by sounds, colours, dances, drama and any other expression of vitality. It is the spirit which the Greeks call Hermes and the Romans Mercurius. Essentially it is the living spirit of Gaia, the earth creature, and all that live upon or within her.

The age of the megalith builders, here equated with the age of the giants, lasted for some 2000 years, from the first settlements in about 4000 B.C. to the coming of solar civilization. It coincided with the astrological age of Taurus the Bull, the sign which corresponds to earth. The religion and magic of that age were, accordingly, based on the powers of earth, and the image of the earth giant was a dominant symbol.

In all previous ages the goddess, Mother Nature, had reigned supreme over Glastonbury Tor. In her aspect as a virgin queen she ruled an unblemished country, never yet raped by ploughmen, miners and quarrymen. Her cycle of fertility was that of the female, associated with the periods of the moon. The primitive year was therefore of thirteen lunar months, each of some 28 days or four 7-day weeks, and the number seven dominated the myths and symbols of that age. The simple tribes followed the seven stars of the Great Bear around the pole of their territory, spun stories out of the wanderings of the seven planets and made music on the seven-toned reed pipe. Seven stages completed the mystery rites of initiation, which took place underground within the womb of the goddess.

Confined below the surface at that time were the goddess's offspring, those mighty forces within the earth which had raised mountains and shaped the features of the landscape. They stirred and rumbled underground, harmless except in occasional earthquakes and eruptions. These were the earth giants, the Titans of Greek mythology. As the tribes settled down in farming communities, the powers of the earth were increasingly invoked. Mother Nature was no longer the sole, supreme deity, for giants appeared on the surface to haunt the lives and imaginations of the neolithic villagers.

The first patron gods of agriculture are described as giants. Typified by the Roman Saturnus, whose emblem was the reaper's sickle, they ruled over simple, pastoral societies, whose possessions were few and superfluous wealth unknown. The golden age had passed, but its afterglow still illuminated those societies, and in later times people looked back nostalgically to the early days under Saturnus. His wife was the archaic earth goddess of Italy, Ops, and his festival of Saturnalia took place at a crucial period of her cycle, over the midwinter solstice. During that period, which is now Christmas, the goddess released into the upper world the monstrous creatures of the abyss, phantoms and anarchical spirits. They were inimical to civilization, and to placate them the Romans at Saturnalia lapsed into an earlier style of life. Laws, warfare and business were suspended, and in the ancient spirit of good cheer presents were exchanged, houses were thrown open to all and servants feasted with their masters.

The character of the giant deity who governed the early Glastonbury farmers is indicated by Plutarch and other Greek writers. They tell of Kronos, one of the Titans, a mythological equivalent of Saturnus. He was lord of the Blessed Islands, and there he maintained the style of the golden age. The souls of the dead were ferried to his realm from the Continent. According to the Greeks, the Blessed Isles were located in the western part of Britain. They could either have been the Scilly Isles or the seven sacred islands of Glastonbury, but Glastonbury alone has the peculiar features and legends which identify it as the former realm of Kronos.

The Glastonbury Kronos was, of course, known by a British name. Almost certainly he was called Bran, a name thunderously appropriate to a giant. Legends of Bran come from all over the British Isles, often with archaic features which imply that he was an aboriginal, pre-Celtic deity. In the old Irish romance, *The Voyage of Bran*, he was guided to the paradisial Blessed Isles to the west, and there like Kronos he finally dwelt. A story in the Welsh *Mabinogion* attributes to him a magic cauldron which revived warriors killed in battle, though leaving them forever speechless. His emblem was the raven, and one of his symbols was a severed head which probably, like John the Baptist's, rested upon a dish. The head of Bran was finally buried in the ancient mound beneath the Tower of London; hence the immemorial practice of keeping ravens at the Tower. While the head was buried there Britain was safe from foreign invasion. King Arthur, it was said, dug it up, wishing to protect the realm by his sword alone. The tradition at the Tower, however, is that while the ravens are there Bran is still the resident guardian.

Ravens are no longer seen over Glastonbury Tor, but they were once plentiful thereabouts, and Bran himself was also indigenous to the area. His legends and symbols point him out as the Grail Keeper, and in that character, under the name of Bron or Brons, he entered the Christian Grail romances, thus continuing his association with Glastonbury.

Prehistoric Glastonbury

Chapter Five
The Gigantic Mysteries of Glastonbury Tor

The mysteries of Glastonbury Tor are not only in its legends but have a physical dimension, openly displayed. The hill is presumed natural, but anyone can see that at one time it has been shaped. Around its sides are several tiers of well defined terraces. They stand out most clearly when the sun is low, but can be seen and walked at any time. It had always been supposed that the terraces were made by early cultivators, for growing vines perhaps.

In 1964 they were seen in an entirely new light by an Irishman, Geoffrey Russell. Twenty years previously he had experienced a vision in which he saw a bilateral figure of concentric rings and understood it to be an image of the brain. Later he came across a diagram of the Cretan labyrinth, as carved on a rock in Tintagel, and recognized it as the figure he had seen in the vision. Labyrinths thereupon became his full-time interest. The subject is notoriously gripping, for the symbolism of the labyrinth is powerful upon a variety of levels. It is generally agreed to be a plan of a journey, a pilgrimage to a world-centre sanctuary such as Jerusalem, and on a deeper level it depicts the pilgrimage of the soul through life, death and rebirth. When Plato in the *Republic* tells of a journey through the afterworld of a soldier who had been left dead on a battlefield, he describes the path of a labyrinth.

When Russell first saw the ringed terraces on Glastonbury Tor he recognized in them the form of a great three-dimensional labyrinth. A survey was made of the Tor and a model of it was constructed, from which it could be seen that the rings were seven in number and joined up to form a continuous pathway towards the top of the Tor, accurately reproducing the twists and turns of the seven-layered labyrinth which symbolized the classical Mysteries.

A discovery of this scale could not immediately be assimilated by archaeologists and Glastonbury scholars. Moreover, like all discoveries at Glastonbury, it came through revelation, which is not a popular medium among the professors. Yet many discerning people have now accepted the reality of the Tor labyrinth; the evidence for it soberly summarized in a booklet by Geoffrey Ashe, and the plain fact of it can be seen by anyone who cares to follow its winding course up the Tor.

In view of Glastonbury Tor's ancient character as Spiral Castle, centre of the Mysteries, the discovery of a spiral labyrinth around its Tor should not be surprising. The interesting question is when it was constructed. The earliest tribes were wholly concerned with keeping their landscape in the same state of nature as they found it. No doubt they regarded the Tor as a place of initiation, but they are not likely to have engraved marks upon it. The labyrinth, then, must have been carved after the time of settlement, from about 4000 B.C. That places it within the age of the giants. It is indeed a typical product of that age. Even though it was always before everyone's eyes, its gigantic scale long hid it from perception. It should perhaps be called the Giant's Maze.

Another gigantic and archaic work involving Glastonbury Tor is the alignment of sanctuaries known as the St Michael line. Geographically it is the longest line across land that can be drawn over southern England, extending from a point near Land's End in the far west to the eastern extremity of East Anglia. On or near its straight course lie major St Michael sanctuaries of western England: Glastonbury Tor, Burrowbridge, Brentor, Roche Rock, St Michael's Mount, Carn Brea (see over).

This alignment is basically a work of nature. Many of its markers, such as the Tor and St Michael's Mount are natural features, but in some period of prehistory the line has been made precise and formal. This is demonstrated most clearly by its central section, beginning at the 'Mump' in Burrowbridge, about twelve miles south-west of Glastonbury. It is a smaller twin of the Tor, a ringed island hill with a ruined church of St Michael on its summit. From the top of the Mump the Tor is visible on the far horizon. The axis of the Mump is aligned on the Tor;

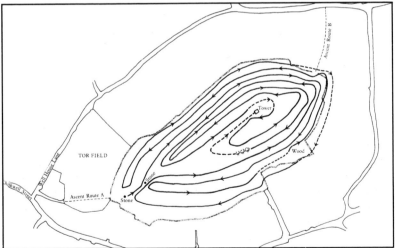

The carved ridges on the flanks of the Tor, most clearly visible from the air, join up to form the pattern of an elongated, seven-ringed labyrinth, as shown in the diagram.

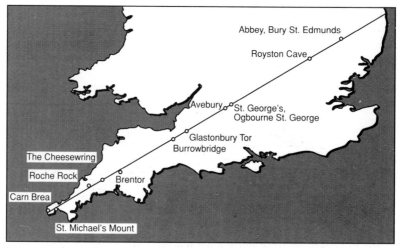

The straight course of the St. Michael Line from the Land's End to the far east of England. The labels refer to St. Michael shrines and other notable sanctuaries lying upon or near it.

its extension marks the old Pilgrims' Way along the Tor's ridge and forms the axis of the labyrinth. Further east the line runs precisely to the main southern entrance to the prehistoric Avebury temple. So it has been calculated by the mathematically adept and obliging Robert Forrest. This straight line continues beyond Avebury to a once important monastic site, the church at Ogbourne St George. St George is said by mystical writers to be the earthly counterpart of St Michael.

In this central section of the St Michael line at least one site is artificial. Avebury is a formal temple, a structure of huge erect stones enclosed by a massive bank and ditch. It was formerly approached by two avenues of standing stones leading to minor temples. The Avebury temple is said to have been erected in the third millenium B.C. It was built within a landscape which nature designed as an Elysium, and it had always been a place of assembly for the early tribes. They held an important yearly festival on Windmill Hill above the Avebury temple.

One thing was, however, lacking at Avebury. There was nothing in its landscape which fittingly represented the world-centre mountain. That deficiency was made good by the erection of Silbury Hill, 130 feet

Silbury Hill (above) and the temple at Avebury enclosed within a moat and earth ramparts. The southern entrance to the temple, on the direct course of the St. Michael line, is on the far side of the ring.

43

Churches on high places, dedicated to the Archangel Michael, guard the ancient pilgrimage route through Glastonbury to the West. St. Michael's church, Brentor, stands upon a moorland rock in Devon.

high and with a base covering 5½ acres. It is not just a great pile of earth but was made permanent by an inner structure of chalk blocks weighing together some million tons. The hill was built at about the same time as the temple and was related to it symbolically and in ritual. Michael Dames in his two books on Avebury and Silbury shows how the natural features and monuments of their neighbourhood formed a miniature sacred landscape, designed to accommodate all the seasonal rites and festivals throughout the year. This indicates that the temple and megalithic complex at Avebury were laid out within an existing sanctuary at a time when the old life of tribal wanderings across a wide countryside had given way to settlement. The year-long tribal pilgrimage was maintained, but on a geographically reduced scale. By priestly art the circuit of spirit shrines around the country was reproduced in one small area, around Avebury. That area became the microcosm of a whole country, inhabited by all its principal gods. Thus it became possible to enjoy the benefits of settlement while continuing to celebrate an annual

St. Michael's church on Burrowbridge Mump is visible from Glastonbury Tor. The Mump is here seen as an island hill once more, surrounded by the floods of early 1990. The spiritual link between these St. Michael sites is apparent from this picture and the photograph of Brentor opposite.

series of festivals as in ancient times. The difference was that all the festivals were now held within the national Elysium.

When the Avebury temple was built, its southern entrance stones were placed accurately on the St Michael line. The alignment already existed, being defined by Glastonbury Tor and the Mump of Burrowbridge. The Mump is presumed to be a natural hill, but certain features of its shape, location and composition suggest otherwise. It is greater in size than Silbury, which is claimed as the largest man-made hill in Europe. If it is artificial, the Mump must surely be one of these unrecognized works of the giant forces commanded by ancient priests.

Further to the west, on the south-east edge of Bodmin Moor, another great landmark stands on the direct course of the St Michael line. The Cheesewring, a towering stack of huge granite slabs balanced one on top of another, is located on the summit of Stow's Hill within a prehistoric stone enclosure. Around it are ancient burials and stone circles. There has long been dispute about the Cheesewring, whether or

One of the gigantic entrance stones at Avebury.

not it is an entirely natural formation. It is difficult to see how nature alone could have contrived it, but it is too vast and rudely shaped to be the unaided work of men. Like the Mump and the maze on Glastonbury Tor, the Cheesewring seems to be a product of the age of giants.

The association with giants which occurs along the St Michael line suggests the presence of earth forces. According to a book recently published, the existence of a geomagnetic energy channel on the course of the line can be detected today and was evidently known in the past. *The Sun and the Serpent* describes a journey of discovery by its two authors, Paul Broadhurst and the Scottish dowser Hamish Miller, along the entire St Michael line. They detected a peculiar form of energy, winding in a serpent fashion around the straight axis of the line, and they were able to trace it from Land's End as far as Avebury. There it made a complicated pattern around the monument and as Hamish Miller followed it with dowsing rods, he was surprised to find that it crossed another energy channel of a different quality. The new current was of opposite, negative charge and thus the counterpart to that of the first channel. Further investigation revealed that there was in fact a double

At Othery church on the St. Michael pilgrimage route, near Burrowbridge, the Archangel is embroidered on a 15th century cope.

line of energy coiling around the St Michael line. The two researchers went back to the beginning and repeated their entire journey up to Avebury, tracking the path of the second channel. They then completed their work by following and mapping the routes of both the energy lines eastward to the North Sea.

The two lines of current which spiral around the straight axis of the St Michael line form the symbol of the serpent-entwined rod of Asclepius, the Greek god of healing. These serpents represent the vital energies around the spine of the human body, and the meaning of the St Michael line is evidently similar. The line marks the backbone of southern England, energized by the vital currents of earth. The sanctuaries on its course where the two currents meet, such as Glastonbury and Avebury, can be seen as the 'chakra' or nodal points in the 'subtle body' of the landscape, its field of geomagnetic and other energies.

Between these places, along the central spine of the country, wound an ancient trackway. It led to the national sanctuary at Avebury, where tribes gathered from afar for seasonal festivals, but it was not primarily a secular route. Every year the course of the line was trodden by certain members of a tribe, those in the process of initiation. A double pathway, one strand leading up the country and the other down, conducted them by wayside shrines to the Mystery centres where the two paths converged. Their guide was the earth spirit, later identified with Hermes whose dual aspect is reflected in the twin, negative and positive currents of the St Michael line. On the high places along the axis of the line, beacon lights were tended by hermits who, as the word implies, were traditional servants of Hermes.

This picture is imaginary, but it is composed of eternal poetic or archetypal images which, before the rise of civilized distractions, dominated the ancient mind and were imitated in the patterns and artifacts of ancient life. A succession of these images was encountered by those who walked the path of initiation. Every district they passed through was known as the scene of certain mythological episodes, and these were illustrated in the hills and folds of the local landscape, brought to life by the interplay of shadows and the light of the sun or moon. As the mythic journey unfolded, it was accompanied by a song which continued throughout its entire course. Thus the pilgrims' way was a chain of poetic images, composed of sun, moon and starlight, hills, vales and springs, local spirits and phantoms, mythological events and the songs of an unbroken linear chant.

In sober fact, there is good evidence of an ancient pilgrims' way approximately on the St Michael line from Cornwall up to Avebury, and the extension of the line eastward follows the general course of the prehistoric Icknield Way into East Anglia. The western part of the line retains local traditions of a former pathway, first trodden by angels. There are even hints of a divine presence on the straight way from the west to the Isle of Avalon. In a book of essays, *Michael, Prince of Heaven*, the seer, Wellesley Tudor Pole, recorded a saying among West Somerset country people, that Jesus once walked the line from St Michael's Mount to Glastonbury, and that one day he will pass that way again. The time and form of his next appearance are unknown, but he must be made welcome, and every traveller should therefore be given hospitality.

During their survey of the St Michael line, Broadhurst and Miller made a remarkable addition to the symbology of Glastonbury Tor. The

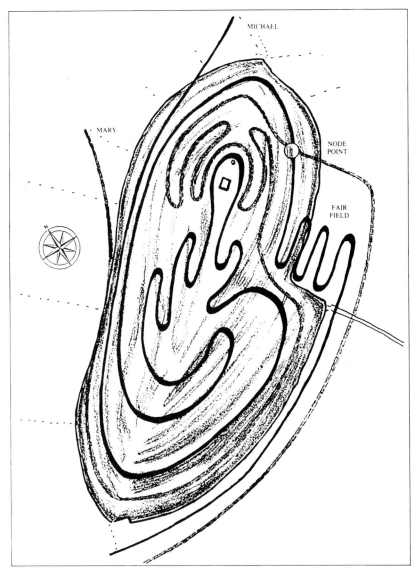

Plan of the Tor, reproduced from The Sun and the Serpent, *showing the positive and negative currents, named Michael and Mary, as traced by Hamish Miller.*

first, positively charged line which they followed made a complicated spiral pattern on the sides of the Tor, including a long, thin loop around its level summit. When they returned to Glastonbury on the trail of the second line of opposite polarity, they found that this too made for the Tor and traced a pattern around it. The main feature of the second design was a bowl-shaped curve around the eastern flank of the hill, opposite the loop formed by the first line. Putting the two shapes together on a plan of the Tor produced a coherent and striking symbol, an image of sexual union, similar in meaning to the combination of light shaft and dark cave which was referred to earlier in connection with megalithic ritual. The discovery on the Tor of this symbol, created by a positive and a negative current of energy, confirms the tradition that Glastonbury Tor was a centre of the ancient mysteries.

Chapter Six
The Giant Killers

The giants of old undoubtedly symbolized natural forces, but we are repeatedly informed by early historians that sometimes they were visible in grotesque and monstrous forms. They belonged, therefore, to the cryptic category of beings which includes the hairy giants or yetis of the Himalayan mountains, the similarly described Sasquatch or Bigfoot of America and our own Loch Ness monster.

These creatures are occasionally seen and heard, and they may appear real to people who encounter them, but essentially they are phantoms. They represent an aspect of the 'genius loci', the indwelling spirit of certain mountains, lakes and wild places. Their forms are fluid and adaptable, being determined by the collective imagination of local people. In traditional societies, magicians and shamans know about such things and are sometimes able to invoke them. In earlier times, it is said, when shamans were more accomplished and could perform feats unknown today, they would summon up the elemental spirits of earth and shape them to their will.

Those who are knowledgeable in the arts of raising spirits and creating thought-forms have written that it is often easier to produce phantoms than to dissolve them. In the course of time they become more solid and may even bleed when wounded. The magicians of the age of Taurus were adept in forming giants and monsters, but like all technologies theirs had unwanted side-effects. Not all the spirits they raised were properly laid to rest, and some lingered about the countryside to establish a breed of monsters. This may be the origin of the giants which, by all accounts, were still to be found in Britain in the second millenium B.C. during the early days of civilization.

The first civilized temple in Britain was Stonehenge, built on the site of an earlier sanctuary at the beginning of the age of Aries in about 2000 B.C. Some of its stones came from far away, and in the first history of Stonehenge by Geoffrey of Monmouth in the twelfth century, the whole monument is said to have been imported by Merlin from Ireland, where it was known as the Giants' Ring because giants of earlier times had brought it there from Africa. The giants had since died out, and with them had died the means of lifting the stones. Merlin was evidently versed in the ancient magical arts, for he easily dismantled the monument, had it loaded in ships for England and set it up on Salisbury Plain.

As the age of Taurus waned and the primitive, elemental magic of the megalith builders gave way to the more subtle variety exemplified by the arts of Merlin, giants became more scarce on the face of the earth. When Brutus, the first king of Britain, landed at Totnes with his Trojan followers, only a few giants were left, and they were mostly confined to the wilds of Cornwall. According to Geoffrey of Monmouth's *History of the Kings of Britain*, one of Brutus' nobles, Corineus, asked to be made governor of Cornwall because his favourite sport was giant hunting. He exterminated all the giants except one, the twelve-foot-tall Gogmagog, and finally killed him also, throwing him off a cliff into the sea.

The downfall of the giants is described mythologically in the story of how Zeus dethroned the Titans and confined them once more below the earth. In historical terms they were destroyed by civilization, together with a new religion which subordinated the earth powers to a solar hierarchy. In Greece, Apollo established the new religion at Delphi, the national sanctuary, transfixing with an arrow the previous guardian of its oracle, a giant earth serpent. Similar feats of killing giants, dragons, huge worms and other forms of earth monster were performed by legendary heroes all over Europe. They are called solar heroes because the civilized religion and social order which they introduced were based on the solar year and the progression of the sun through the twelve signs of the zodiac.

The British version of Apollo, the god or hero who revealed the secrets of the zodiacal civilization to the tribes of Glastonbury, was

The legendary builder of Stonehenge, as depicted in a 14th century manuscript. Merlin, the giant wizard, makes light of raising one of the lintel stones.

undoubtedly Arthur. In the mythology of the solar religion he played the part of the sun. The new religion superseded the cult of earth powers, and wherever it was implanted the giants were expelled. Arthur slew the ogre of Mont St Michel, and from Glastonbury he sent an expedition against the giants of Brent Knoll, the prominent hill visible from the Tor to the north-west. In the story given by William of Malmesbury, one of Arthur's knights, Yder, went on ahead and killed the giants single-handed, but was himself mortally wounded. In his memory Arthur gave riches to Glastonbury Abbey and established there an order of 24 monks.

The mention here of Glastonbury Abbey is, of course, an anachronism. In the early days of the Abbey the local pagan kings were probably known as Arthur, for the Celtic high king represented Arthur the sun god. The title was inherited by the first Christian rulers, notably by that fifth-century King Arthur mentioned in the old chronicles. His legend, however, derived for the most part from that of Arthur the god and thus from the beginning of the Celtic culture in Britain. The legends of giant-killing certainly date from that period. There are widely different opinions as to when the Celtic culture entered Britain, but if it is equated with solar civilization, the first evidence of it is Stonehenge, a solar orientated, twelve-god temple, built in about 2000 B.C. This does not

Brent Knoll, a prominent feature in the Glastonbury landscape, a prehistoric fortress, and the location of an episode in the local Arthurian legend.

mean that the whole country was converted at that time to the new religion. For many hundreds of years the old earth cults survived, and the giants still haunted the wilder parts of Britain.

The story of Brutus can be seen as a foundation legend of the Celtic culture. He was advised by a council of twelve elders, headed by a chief augur, and he finished off the remaining giants. Thus he may typify the Celtic warrior-missionaries who, from the beginning of the second millenium B.C., brought the solar religion to Britain. The supposed date of Brutus' arrival was after the fall of Troy in about 1,200 B.C. This is likely to have been about the time when the new religion and the twelve-part, zodiacal order of Celtic society became prevalent throughout most of the country.

The battle against giants, as conducted by the solar heroes, was on two levels: first, materially, it meant defeating or converting tribes who still practised the neolithic earth cults, and on another level it was a magical war against phantom earth monsters. Not anyone could kill giants, only those with the proper knowledge and equipment. As creatures of magic they had to be destroyed by magic of a higher order.

In Celtic and earlier times, warfare was conducted to a large extent on a magical plane. The ancient Irish histories tell of rival Druids raising storms and demons against each other and creating 'glamour' or illusions to confuse the enemy. Giants sometimes appeared in these battles. They were of great might, but theirs were the dark powers of the earth, and the new, solar order was armed more effectively with the power of light. Arthur's sword, Excalibur, is recognized as a solar instrument. Like the swords of the Vikings and the Japanese samurai, it was wrought by initiated craftsmen during a process of ritual, and was charged with the electric energies of the sun. Every Celtic tribe possessed its own magical sword. Armed with such a weapon, a brave man could challenge giants and earth dragons, and often, though not always, defeat them.

The triumph of solar, Bronze Age magic and civilization over the neolithic earth sorcery foreshadowed another victory of light over darkness, which took place some 2000 years later, at the beginning of the succeeding Piscean age, when Christianity supplanted a degenerate paganism.

Prehistoric Glastonbury

Chapter Seven
Arthur the Sun King
and the Zodiacal Round Table

The Age of Aries which followed Taurus and the neolithic age of giants is known to prehistorians as the Bronze Age, because burials from that period contain metalwork of a type and quality previously unknown. Powerful new weapons, bronze daggers, swords, axes and armour, are included among them, together with splendid items of priestly regalia, such as the gold torques found mostly in Ireland, and rich personal ornaments—armlets, bracelets, amber necklaces, brooches and ear-rings. Many such items, discovered near or under the causeways through the Glastonbury peat bogs, are displayed in Somerset museums. With them is evidence of expert craftsmanship in other materials, in carpentry, carving, pottery and weaving. The products of these crafts, from chariots and farm carts to pins, buttons and carved bone combs, were skilfully decorated with geometric designs which clearly derived from a scholarly tradition. These relics show the material and cultural opulence of the Celtic civilization which flourished through the Bronze Age and, with declining artistic standards, into the Iron Age up to the first centuries A.D. Time, unfortunately, has destroyed the fabrics, robes, hangings and carpets of that period, whose subtle colours and patterns can now only be imagined.

Ritual objects in gold and bronze are solar symbols, and the beginning of the Bronze Age in Britain coincided with the appearance of a new religion, centred on the sun. That event was marked by the

A bronze shield found in the River Thames, typifying the artistry and craft of Bronze Age Britain.

rebuilding of Stonehenge, converting it from a lunar-orientated shrine to a temple aligned with midsummer sunrise. Commenting on the Bronze Age solar alignments in his book, *The Stonehenge People*, Aubrey Burl writes that "such orientations were the result of a developing cult of the sun among societies in which the fires of metalworking smiths, the rippling gold of molten copper and the eye-blinding brilliance of the sun may have mingled in a rich, entrancing solar cosmology quite unlike the cold, lunar mysticism of Neolithic people". The form of that cosmology and of the solar religion and society that went with it, can be reconstructed from the evidence of a world-wide tradition.

The solar civilization was built upon an esoteric code of law. Essentially it was a code of number, representing the mathematics of creation, and from it were derived all the art forms and institutions of the nation, its music, the proportions of its temples and even its constitution. Plato referred to it in the *Laws* and was curious to know how it originated. He asked his fellow sages in other countries, and the answer was in every case the same. Their law, they all said, was first revealed to them by a god.

Plato's own account of how civilized culture began was that the gods themselves once reigned on earth, and when they departed they initiated certain people into the secrets of their law. As long as the divine standards were upheld, society flourished, but gradually human rulers became lax. Decadence crept in, civilization grew corrupt and was thereafter doomed to fall.

The gods who formerly ruled were twelve in number, each of them governing a certain part of the world and one of the twelve sectors of every country. When they departed, the practice of dividing countries into twelve parts, centred on the national sanctuary, was long maintained. The people of a nation were made into twelve tribes, and each occupied one of the twelve sectors which corresponded to the twelve gods, zodiacal signs and months of the year. The tribes were ruled by twelve kings who claimed descent from the original gods. Four of the kings were paramount in each of the four quarters of the country, and at the centre was a high king whose office was sometimes filled by one of the twelve kings in turn. The whole state was designed as a zodiac circle, imitating the zodiacal wheel of the heavens.

Examples of twelve-tribe, zodiacal societies have been found universally. Best known is the league of twelve Israelite tribes under King Solomon. Also recorded are the numerous twelve-tribe *amphictyonies* (federations of tribes sharing a common sanctuary) of ancient Greece and Asia Minor, including those of Delphi, Athens and Delos. Similar organizations were formed in Italy by the Etruscans, in Gaul, Ireland and all the Celtic countries and throughout Scandinavia under the twelve gods of Odin. When Iceland was first settled, during the ninth and tenth centuries, the new colonists, who were mainly Scandinavian with an admixture of Celts, formed their constitution on the traditional model, dividing the whole island first into four and then twelve units, establishing a sacred centre round a prominent rock and holding national assemblies there each year.

A detailed summary of the zodiacal societies which have been known all over the world is given in a previous book, *Twelve-Tribe Nations* (written in collaboration with Christine Rhone), where examples are found in America, the Pacific islands, China, India, Mesopotamia and elsewhere in the East, in ancient Egypt, among the Ashanti and other nations of Africa and in Madagascar, where a typical twelve-tribe, twelve-king constitution lasted up to the end of the nineteenth century when it was destroyed by colonialism. A feature of all such societies is that they are seen in retrospect as the high point of civilization, the great age of every culture. Plato in the *Laws* gives the formula of an ideal twelve-tribe state and recommends it as the best possible form of government.

These societies were not static but were designed to reflect the cycle of the seasons and the progress of the sun through the zodiac. They also preserved the pattern of former nomadic times when the tribes made a circuit of their territory in the course of each year. The result was a cosmologically ordered civilization which incorporated the spiritual values of the old wandering life.

In each of the twelve tribal sections were instituted festivals at different times and places, one for every day of the year, the cycle of festivals proceeding round the country like the hand of a clock. Each one was different in character, being appropriate to the ruling god of the region where it was held as well as to the spirits of its locality. These festivals were occasions of religious ceremony, bardic recital, judgement and law-giving and, on a popular level, of games, competitions, trading and social intercourse. Certain songs and stories were associated with every festival. The climax of the year remained as it had been in primitive times, the grand convention of all the tribes at the national Elysium.

The most influential of all the arts is music. This was recognized by the law-givers who first prescribed the songs and chants which were heard at each festival. They were based in every district on the traditional music of the countryside, reformed and codified. The music of early times, as played on the shepherd's reed pipe, derived from the seven-tone scale. With the coming of civilization and the twelve-tribe order of society, the scale was amplified into twelve notes from which came the classical twelve-tone chant of temple and church music. The twelve tones corresponded to the twelve signs of the zodiac and were allotted to each part of the country according to the sign that ruled it. Thus the twelve tribes of a nation were bound to a zodiac wheel, animated throughout the year by a constant round of chanting. It can be imagined that when the tribes assembled for their main annual festival, twelve choirs came together to perform the full twelve-part chant of their national music.

The national music accompanied a national myth which was likewise divided into twelve parts and apportioned round the twelve sectors of the country. It described the adventurous journey of a solar hero through the twelve signs of the zodiac, and consisted therefore of twelve principal episodes. Known examples include the twelve-part epics of Gilgamesh, Hercules, Samson, Odysseus and, in Celtic countries, Arthur.

In the zodiacal myth King Arthur played the part of the sun; he fought twelve battles, defeated twelve kings and ruled over a twelve-nation kingdom. These legends once belonged to a twelve-part mythic cycle which was settled upon all the Celtic twelve-tribe landscapes and progressed month by month through the twelve zodiacal sectors. As the myth reached each sector, King Arthur's court would appear. It was represented by a splendidly dressed party of travellers, including noble-men, judges and their officers, bards, story-tellers, singers and entertain-ers, who presided over the round of meetings and festivals. That was the original time of carnival, when life took on a mythological flavour, disputes were settled, fates were decided and the local year reached its festive climax.

The Arthurian mythic cycle has left its mark on the traditions of many Celtic landscapes. Among the Glastonbury locations of Arthur's legend are the site of the former Meare Pool where he received Excalibur from the Lady of the Lake; Pomparles Bridge, between Glastonbury and Street, where the Lady repossessed it; Beckery island where he had a mystical experience in the Chapel Perilous; his fortress on the Tor; the rival fortress of his giant adversary on Brent Knoll; his palace at South Cadbury and his burial place in the Abbey graveyard.

The ancient Pomparles Bridge, a monument with Arthurian associations on the road from Glastonbury to Street.

These associations may not all be old, for legends have a tendency to shift their ground, but the wealth of Arthurian lore which is retained in the Glastonbury landscape indicates that the country within and around the Twelve Hides was once the setting for a complete, twelve-part cycle of King Arthur's myth.

This seems to be confirmed by a note at the end of *The High History of the Holy Graal*, as translated by Sebastian Evans from the thirteenth-century French *Perceval le Gallois ou le conte du Graal*. It reads:

> "The Latin from whence this History was drawn into Romance, was taken in the Isle of Avalon, in a holy house of religion that standeth at the head of the Moors Adventurous, there where King Arthur and Queen Guinevere lie."

Thus we are told that the episodes of the Arthur cycle were indeed located around Glastonbury.

Glastonbury's mythological landscape is far from unique. Not only South Cadbury but Winchester, Carlisle and other places in Scotland, England, Wales, Cornwall and Brittany are reasonably claimed as the site where Arthur held court at Camelot. Many separate regions are imbued with Arthurian legend. Around Carlisle, for example, are places known as Arthur's Chair, his Chamber, Well, Round Table and the cavern where he sleeps. This widespread distribution of Arthurian lore and place-names clearly predates the Dark Ages when a semi-historical King Arthur rallied the Britons against Saxon invaders. It implies that other parts of the country besides Glastonbury had twelve-tribe, zodiacal societies, inhabiting districts where the various scenes in a year-long epic of Arthur and his twelve knights were associated with local landmarks.

Every landscape where a nation of twelve tribes lived under the spell of the King Arthur story was a model of the Round Table. Glastonbury is an obvious example. The Round Table, laid out in the form of a zodiac over the country around the Tor, was the conceptual creation of a civilization which appears to have risen some 4000 years ago, at the beginning of the age of Aries. Its religion was based on a solar myth within the twelve-part framework of the zodiac, and the leader of its

South Cadbury castle with its massive ramparts, drawn by William Stukeley in the 18th century.

twelve ruling gods was a British version of Apollo, namely Arthur.

The origins of Glastonbury's Round Table lie in times before civilization, when Arthur was Arcturus, the keeper of the Great Bear formed by Glastonbury's seven sacred islands. With solar civilization came a highly structured social order, dominated throughout by the number twelve. The earthly Round Table was converted from a stellar landscape into a giant zodiac with twelve sectors round the Isle of Avalon, and Arthur with twelve companion knights was recast as a solar hero. The Great Bear was then seen as the vehicle in which the sun god circled the heavens. Thus it acquired its old English name—Arthur's chariot.

In the Chinese book of historical records, the *Shih Chi*, compiled in about the second century B.C., the Great Bear is said to be the chariot of the heavenly ruler, the pole star. Known to the Chinese as the Bushel, this constellation was seen as the hand of a celestial clock. As the Great Bear circles the pole, the three stars in its tail point outwards, providing an indication of the seasons. Chinese astronomers observed the stars at nightfall, and noted that the tail of the Bear points to the south in the summer, the west in autumn, the north in winter and the east in spring. In the words of the *Shih Chi*, "the Bushel is the car of the ruler, revolving in the central region of the sky, visiting and ordering the four directions, dividing light and darkness, settling the four seasons, equalizing the five elements, regulating periods and degrees, and fixing the various calculations of the calendar".

As the heavens were seen as the dial of a great clock, so also was the surface of the earth. According to the Sinologist, Dr Chalmers (quoted in W.E. Soothill's *Hall of Light*), the horizon was divided into twelve parts, making due north the centre of the first division. This procured a zodiacal lay-out of the landscape, corresponding to the Arthurian Round Table.

The Glastonbury landscape is like an ancient document whose original inscriptions have been amended and added to by the scribes of many ages. At one time it was divided into twelve sectors in the image of Arthur's Round Table. An even earlier pattern was formed by alignments of Stone Age sites, probably making pilgrimage routes, which converged upon the Tor. With the Christian foundation, the sacred geography of Glastonbury was reinterpreted in accordance with the legend of the Twelve Hides.

Even though it has been marked over thousands of years by different forms of religion and society, the Glastonbury landscape has developed in organic fashion, the sacred features of previous ages being included within later schemes. The area contains two of the best authenticated alignments in southern England, the St Michael line examined in Chapter Five and another, shown on the map overleaf, which runs approximately north-south through the Tor. This second line is found to provide one of the sides of a square, 1440 acres in area, centred upon the site of St Joseph's original church at Glastonbury.

This area of 1440 acres is also equal to twelve hides (a Somerset hide being commonly of 120 acres, though 160 acres and other values are known). Here, then, are the Twelve Hides of Glastonbury. The side of a square containing twelve hides measures exactly twelve furlongs. This reveals the symbolic meaning of the Twelve Hides, for in Revelation 21, the Heavenly Jerusalem, the image of paradise on earth described by St. John, had a side measuring 12,000 furlongs, a thousand times the measure of the Twelve Hides.

From whatever angle one studies the Glastonbury mystery, the direction in which one is led is always the same; and finally one is confronted with a now unfamiliar archetype, an ancient ever-living idea which finds no recognition in the secular world-view, the archetype of an Earthly Paradise. It is the ultimate reference of all the Glastonbury legends and romances, and its image is marked upon the Avalonian countryside.

On this map of Glastonbury and its surroundings shown overleaf, some of the hypothetical twelve divisions are indicated by existing features, such as the two old roads which enter the square of the Twelve Hides by its northern corners. One diagonal of the square extends precisely to Wells Cathedral, through the market cross, and continues parallel to the old road over the Mendips; the other diagonal points to Meare and follows the lines of roads and waterways in the direction of Brent Knoll.

For some of the other divisions there is little or no evidence, and different arrangements can be contemplated; but this scheme typifies the twelve-part zodiacal ordering of landscapes in Celtic and other solar civilizations.

The twelve sectors of the landscape formed an extensive circle, known as the Round Table, which reflected the heavenly order and thus attracted divine blessings. Some of its features were archaic but its completion as a zodiacal wheel dates from the early Celtic period when Arthur was the sun god and the Great Bear his chariot.

Glastonbury's native god and hero has gone through many changes, adapting himself to the spirit of every age. Beginning as Arcturus in a stellar mythology, he rose to splendour as the Celtic sun god and inserted himself into Christianity, both esoterically through the Celtic mysteries and, publicly, as the ideal example of a chivalrous Christian prince.

Through all his transformations Arthur has retained something of his original character. At every stage he has represented an aspiration which remains constant in the human soul, for a return to the natural conditions of the golden age. The innocent days of tribal wanderings have gone beyond recall, but as lord of Glastonbury's Round Table, Arthur conducted the quest for a new golden age under conditions of civilization. The symbol of that quest is the Grail, and its last appearance upon earth was during the period of zodiacal order, when the country was held under the enchantment of myth and music, as Arthur and his solar court moved with the seasons through the twelve divisions of the landscape. In the course of time the enchantment dissolved and, as happened to the Greek *amphictyonies* around the sixth century B.C., the twelve-tribe social structure fell apart. Arthur then became a revivalist, leading his twelve knights on the quest which has continued to this day, for the restoration of the Grail and the renewal of divine government on earth. It is, perhaps, not so much a quest as a vigil, for the legend that Arthur lies sleeping beneath a hill near Glastonbury, and simultaneously in other caves about the country, suggests that he is awaiting a new revelation which will come inevitably when the times are ready for it.

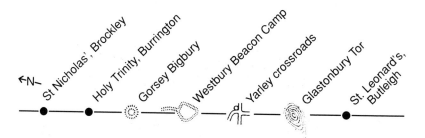

The Twelve Hides or 1440 acres of Glastonbury can be drawn as a square, centred on the site of the Old Church, with a side measuring 1½ miles (the tinted area on the map opposite). The eastern side of the square is defined by the line of sites (reproduced above after Devereux and Thompson's Ley Hunter's Companion*) running north from Butleigh church through the church tower on the Tor. The other sides and the extended diagonals of the square are linked to ancient sites and monuments in the Glastonbury area. By this figure the countryside around the square Twelve Hides is divided into twelve sectors bordering the Twelve Hides themselves.*

Also shown, by a broken line, is the path of a vestigial ancient trackway which runs straight between the site of the old chapel on Godney Island and the Old Church on the Isle of Avalon, continuing to the site of Butleigh church. The straight stretch of causeway, now a road, from Godney to the former Godney lake village (marked X) defines the line which, extended northwards, points to a peak of the Mendips.

The dotted line represents the St. Michael line, passing over the Tor and through the south-west corner of the Twelve Hides square.

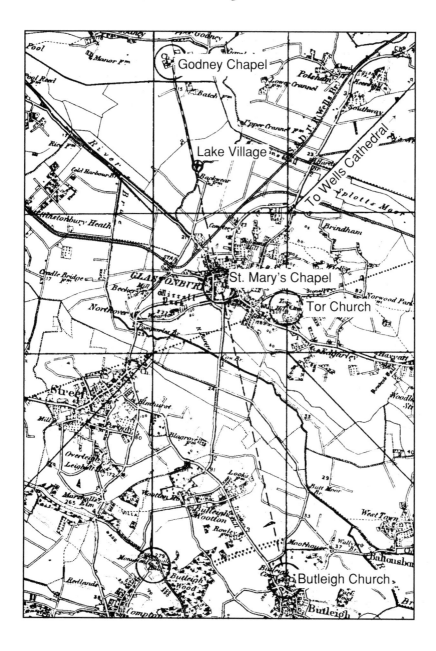

Prehistoric Glastonbury

Chapter Eight
Life and Religion in the Kingdom of Arthur

The social order established at Glastonbury in early Celtic times continued for at least 3,000 years to influence the local economy and customs. From the second millenium B.C., when the solar religion with Arthur and twelve zodiacal gods was first introduced, until the destruction of the Abbey in 1539 A.D., Glastonbury was almost always under the rule of a religious authority. About halfway through that period pagan doctrines and Druidry gave way to Christianity, but the lives of ordinary people were largely unaffected by the change. The methods by which the Glastonbury monks administered the Twelve Hides could scarcely have differed much from those used by their predecessors in the former Druid college on the Isle of Avalon.

There are no records of Glastonbury life before the Middle Ages, but a document which survived the fall of the Abbey gives a detailed picture of the local economy in the last years of monastic rule. In the old Abbey book of rents and customs are the names of all who held land within the Twelve Hides, and on what terms. The peculiar rights of each tenant were noted, such as where, when and what kind of game he was allowed to hunt, the number and types of animals he could graze on the common, the amount of land he could cultivate, where he could cut turves, catch fish and so on. To all these rights were attached certain rents, tithes or duties. A holder of Abbey lands might have been required to give a portion of his labour, skills or produce to the officers who managed the Abbey estates. He might have been charged with the maintenance of a certain stretch of road or waterway, navigating the abbot's barge, helping with the annual wine or cider making or providing a certain dish for an Abbey feast. Many of the Abbey offices were hereditary, certain families specializing in certain departments of the local economy, such as the Abbey fisheries and beehives, the conservation of game and woodlands and the maintenance of buildings. So respectful of custom and ancient usage were people of that time that it is not impossible that some of the servants of the medieval Abbey were continuing a family tradition, unbroken since the days when Glastonbury's Twelve Hides were administered by a Chief Druid.

The picturesque muddle of feudal rights and duties on the medieval Glastonbury estates was the delayed relic of the more rational, principled system which was instituted by the early Celtic civilization. From known examples of solar, duodecimally ordered societies, and from Plato's descriptions of their archetype in the *Laws* and *Republic*, it can be assumed that all the lands within the Twelve Hides, apart from the central sanctuary, were divided, first into quarters, then into twelve regions, and finally in equally productive portions between the heads of each local family. The duties of each individual, to his family, clan, village, region, quarter and community as a whole, as well as to the gods who ruled it, were clearly defined. Everyone had his prescribed functions in an order of society which was designed to reflect the order of the heavens, and the supreme ruler was a king who represented the sun. Uniformity was the most obvious principle in that society. The whole nation shared the same religion and customs and was influenced by the same forms of myth and music. Regulation was applied even to the number and standard sizes of kitchen utensils in every household.

In the earliest, simplest form of solar civilization, the twelve regional chiefs met together in annual council, each of them presiding in turn. At that stage there were no permanent national institutions; order was maintained by the power of myth and music alone. When the population increased and affairs became more complicated, an administrative high king was appointed. Thereafter, as towns and villages developed and society could no longer be governed by the simple principles of its founders, a national council of representatives met to advise the king and began to assume many of the ruling functions. In Plato's account of this later stage, the council consisted of thirty delegates from each of the

The 14th-century Fish House at Meare, another of the seven islands, was built on the edge of Meare Lake. The lake is now dry except in times of flood. Formerly it provided fish for the Abbey and the inhabitants of the Twelve Hides. The Fish House was the office and residence of the Piscator, or head fisherman to the Abbey.

twelve regions, making up a ruling body of 360 members. Each group of thirty governed for one month in the year.

Every village and region was similarly governed by a council of representatives, but there was no democracy in the modern sense, for elections were not general, but were held at each level among chiefs of equal rank who chose representatives from among their own number to serve on higher councils. There was also a caste system which ensured that only members of certain families could hold positions of power. The religious authorities in Plato's state were the Guardians, a chaste and vegetarian body of initiated scholars. In Celtic societies, the Guardians' functions were performed by the Druids, and thus one can suppose that the affairs of Glastonbury's Twelve Hides were formerly managed by a college of Druids, the pagan prototype of Glastonbury Abbey.

The Celtic solar civilization gave security and continuity within a well ordered, self-perpetuating society, but at the expense of individual freedom. For better or for worse, everyone was closely integrated within the social order, having certain defined responsibilities and corresponding privileges. In this system can be found elements of both fascism and communism, but neither of those terms properly apply to it, for the solar society was not based on any secular ideal, but took as its model the plan of the heavens, divided between the twelve signs of the zodiac. The key to interpreting the celestial plan came through divine revelation. It involved an esoteric understanding of number and the adoption of a numerical standard, constituting the national code of law. Music, as we have already seen, was the chief expression of that law, and the music and myth of the King Arthur cycle were the most powerful influence in the lives of those inhabiting the pre-Christian Twelve Hides. It is impossible, therefore, to compare the zodiacal constitution of the ancient Celts with any political system known today, for its laws were not arbitrary but were based on divinely established principles, and it was upheld, not so much by coercion as by a form of musical enchantment.

Enchantments tend to fade with time. Plato promised that the ideal, twelve-tribe state would last just as long as its laws and customs were rigorously adhered to. Human nature, however, is not adapted to keeping things in the same constant condition. Many of the rules in the ancient order, such as those governing marriage and child-raising, though designed astrologically for the benefit of society, must often have conflicted with people's own ideas about whom they wanted to marry and when their children should be born. One can imagine how kind officials bent the rules to oblige individuals, how variations crept into the chants and stories, how certain customs were neglected... and how the system gradually dissolved, becoming more human and earthly and less effectively enchanted in the process.

The most apparent cause of social dissolution was the invention of money and the rise of commerce. Riches from trade were the downfall of the twelve-tribe societies throughout Greece and the Mediterranean. Their dissolution took place around the sixth century B.C., and since Britain had long been exposed to Mediterranean traders, the decline of its enchantment probably began at about the same time. Archaeology provides firm evidence of this. In the last few centuries before Christ the peoples of the Somerset Levels grew more numerous and had access to foreign luxuries. They imported fine wines from the Continent, and their possessions, including delicate flagons, chalices and wine strainers, give signs of lordly feasts. Glastonbury's waterways, far more extensive than they are now, provided harbours for sea-going vessels and trade routes into the interior. At the same time, Glastonbury lay at the junction of the main trackways to and from the West Country. Minerals, skins and other native produce were brought there from many parts of Britain for bartering with foreign merchants. Margaret Deanesly, in her account of *The Pre-Conquest Church in England,* describes the trading port of Glastonbury at the beginning of the Christian era as "the Bristol of its day".

Throughout the centuries of dissolution, as trade flourished and the ancient social structure decayed, the Druids retained their influence and kept up a semblance of the old order. Up to the time when Britain was occupied by the Romans, they supervised the division of land, ensuring that certain plots in every village were set aside for the relief of the aged and indigent, for common expenses and tithes. They also administered the sacred lands, which included the major sanctuaries with temples and colleges, such as Glastonbury, and the sites of many of today's parish churches, where modest shrines were concealed in groves of oak and yew. A sure sign of Druid influence is in the statement of a fifth-century Roman author, that the Dumnonians, the Celtic nation of the West Country to which the Glastonbury tribes belonged, had no coinage, refused to handle money and insisted on dealing only by exchange of goods.

Probably soon after the Roman invasion of 43 A.D. the Celtic college at Glastonbury was suppressed, together with all the religious functions of the Druids. With the collapse of their authority many people were left in confusion. In place of the former religion Mithraic and other cults arose, some native and some of Roman origin. It was an age of prophecies and millennial excitement, and the spirit of the times had a radical effect upon the Druids. In the countries where they still held sway, in Ireland and the outlying parts of Britain, they underwent a reformation.

History has nothing to say of this period, so the causes of the Druid reformation are beyond certain knowledge. There is a strong suggestion that it was inspired, not only by the upheavals of the age but principally by the influence of astrology and the sacred calendar. The age of Pisces was dawning, and such periods of astrological change are traditionally marked by disturbances, portents and changes in human thought patterns, leading to new religious forms and expressions. The Druids were naturally aware of this, both from the astrological calendar and by observing the upheavals around them, and they prepared themselves for the revelation in Pisces. Many prophets and cult leaders were competing for supremacy at that crucial period, but Christ prevailed; and when the light of Christianity first illuminated Britain, the Druids were found ready to receive it.

PART II:
THE CHRISTIAN REVELATION

Chapter Nine
The Glastonbury Legend

The legend of Glastonbury is that, shortly after the Crucifixion, twelve holy men from the East, led by St Joseph of Arimathea, came to Glastonbury and founded there the first church in Britain—or in all Christendom. History neither confirms nor refutes this story, but it does record that Christianity was established in Britain at a very early date, compatible with the legendary date of St Joseph's mission. In about 200 A.D., Tertullian wrote that by his time "parts of Britain inaccessible to the Romans were conquered by Christ", and this was confirmed by his contemporary, Origen, the early Christian Father, who made several references to an established Church among the Britons. The most scrupulous of early British chroniclers, St Gildas in the fourth century, asserted that Christianity came to Britain during the reign of the Roman emperor Tiberias, which ended in 37 A.D.

Critics of Glastonbury's early foundation legend point out that Irenaeus, Bishop of Lyons in the second century, who drew up a list of all Christian churches, made no mention of Britain. It is unlikely, however, that Irenaeus would have included the Celtic Church on his list, for he was a stern opponent of heresies and deviations from Rome, and from the Roman point of view the Church in Britain was an heretical, semi-pagan institution. Perhaps the most telling argument for the early origin of the British Church is that, at the Council of Arles in 314, three British bishops were present, those of London, Caerleon and York, and at subsequent Church councils it was the custom to give precedence to the British representatives because of Glastonbury's claim to be the site of the first Christian church, founded by St Joseph.

It was the fashion among scholars of a previous generation to equate scepticism with respectability and to denigrate such old-established legends such as that of St Joseph at Glastonbury. Yet modern authors can scarcely pretend to know better than their learned predecessors, from the fourth century through the Middle Ages, who had access to documents, now destroyed and forgotten, which persuaded them that at Glastonbury was founded the first church in Christendom. It is significant that during the Middle Ages, when churches and abbeys were vying with each other in their claims to early and impressive foundations, the traditional priority of Glastonbury was never challenged.

At the opposite extreme to the sceptics are the partisans of the Glastonbury legend. They have included mystical nationalists, British Israelites, Druid revivalists and Protestant reformers, but historical evidence is not discredited by the theories of enthusiasts, and many learned authors who have surveyed the evidence of St Joseph at Glastonbury have been inclined to believe it. Some have gone further and improved the legend by adding more impressive episodes. In his book of 1860, *St Paul in Britain*, Rev. R.W. Morgan, who was prominent among the Welsh Druids of his time, presented the evidence for missions to Britain, not only by Paul but by Simon Zelotes, St Peter and other notable figures of early Christianity. There is more evidence, he said, for Paul's foundation of the the British Church than for St Peter at Rome.

The most compelling of modern writers who have taken a positive view of the matter was the Rev. Lionel Smithett Lewis, Vicar of Glastonbury in the 1920s and '30s. His *St Joseph of Arimathea at Glastonbury*, first published in 1922, was expanded through many editions and is still in print. It provided scholarly backing for the mystical revival which had been developing at Glastonbury since early in the century, when Frederick Bligh Bond began his inspired excavations in the Abbey ruins. Lewis's aim was to revive the spirit of Celtic Christianity within the Church of England. As he saw it, not only the Church, but all traditional institutions of Britain, including the monarchy, derived their legitimacy from St Joseph's mission. Up to the time of Henry VIII, English kings were proud to trace their descent through King Arthur from Joseph of Arimathea, and many of them made pilgrimages to Glastonbury. As a way of renewing this link, Lewis started the pleasant custom whereby the Vicar of Glastonbury provides the king or queen of the day with a flowering sprig of the Glastonbury thorn each Christmas.

Two other clergymen, H.A. Lewis, author of *Christ in Cornwall*, and Cyril Dobson of *Did Our Lord Visit Britain as they say in Cornwall and Somerset?* joined forces with the Vicar of Glastonbury in expanding the Glastonbury legend. From evidence found in place names, folklore and old miners' traditions in West Cornwall and at Priddy on the Mendips, they came to believe that, concealed behind the story of St Joseph's foundation of Glastonbury, lay an even more impressive truth. A legend of St Joseph is that he was a merchant. He may have sailed to Britain for cargoes of Cornish tin, and he may have brought his young nephew, Jesus, with him. H.A. Lewis, Vicar of St Martins, one of the Isles of Scilly, collected traces of this legend from fourteen different spots on the Cornish coasts and moorlands. The Cornish legend had previously been noticed by the nineteenth-century folklore collector, Sabine Baring Gould. In his *Book of Cornwall* he recorded the belief among tin miners that Jesus himself, on a visit to Britain with St Joseph, had taught their ancient predecessors how to extract tin from the rock. Every time the tin was 'flashed', one of the miners would shout, "Joseph was in the tin trade!"

Rev. Dobson discovered other such legends in Somerset. A popular expression among country people on the Mendips, "As sure as our Lord was at Priddy!", derived from the local belief that Jesus had passed over those hills on his way to Glastonbury. Also recorded was an old story of how Jesus and St Joseph came to the Summer Land in a ship of Tarshish and stayed at a place called Paradise. Glastonbury is the ancient Elysium or Paradise of the Summer Land, and the name still haunts its locality; there is an area called Paradise at the west end of the town, as well as a Paradise Farm and Paradise Lane north of the Tor. Dobson concluded that Jesus had indeed visited Glastonbury, and he traced his route from the Bristol Channel at Burnham, where he found another Paradise name, to the Isle of Avalon by way of the river Brue.

An "old legend of poetry", quoted in F. J. Snell's *King Arthur's*

Country, reflects the local tradition that St Joseph, possibly with Jesus, journeyed to Glastonbury over the Mendips from a port on the Bristol Channel, near the mouth of the river Parrett. Its first two lines are:

"The good saint Arimathean Joseph, borne by the
Parrett's tide
To Combwich, o'er the Mandips at length he came
to Glaston's hide."

The tradition of Jesus's presence at Glastonbury is certainly ancient, for it is implied in the earliest chronicles, beginning with the Life of St Dunstan, written at the end of the tenth century and containing the first extant reference to the Glastonbury foundation legend. Its anonymous author stated that the wattle church was not built by human hands but was the work of Christ himself, who dedicated it to the Virgin Mary. This is repeated in the legend of St David, who proposed to rededicate the church after he had enlarged it in the sixth century. He was warned by Jesus in a dream that he himself had already dedicated it to his Mother.

The church at Glastonbury could therefore have been founded by Jesus himself. That would explain the mystical epithets applied to it in ancient ecclesiastical documents, 'The House of God' and 'The Secret of the Lord', and it would give good reason for the remarkable reputation which Glastonbury enjoyed from the earliest times throughout Christendom. Dobson and his colleagues suggested that Jesus was at Glastonbury during his 'hidden years'—the period of his life about which nothing is known—before entering upon his mission at the age of thirty. In that case Glastonbury was the fount and origin of Christianity. If Jesus went to the Celtic Mysteries centre on the Isle of Avalon to study the esoteric science in which he later revealed himself to be an adept, his initiators would have been the Druids. Among them at that time were the most learned men in Europe, and their colleges in Britain and Ireland were the last to offer the traditional form of mystical education, attracting pupils from all over the Continent.

One can pleasantly imagine that Jesus came to Glastonbury for his final religious education, and that his doctrine of love supported by knowledge was formulated—as William Blake also imagined—"upon

Bligh Bond's reconstruction of St. Joseph's church at Glastonbury with the cells of the original twelve missionaries.

England's mountains green". Glastonbury Tor and the slopes of Avalon seem an appropriate setting. If Jesus attended the Celtic college at Glastonbury, that would make sense of an otherwise inexplicable feature of early Christianity in Britain, the remarkable similarity between its rites and doctrines and those of the Druids. Those who are inclined to accept Jesus as a graduate of Glastonbury will also find truth in Blake's further assertions, that the Jews learnt their religion from the Druids, and that: "All things begin and end in Albion's ancient Druid rocky shore."

Another possibility raised by the clergymen was that the Virgin Mary had been at Glastonbury, and had died there. Celtic churches were dedicated to the saint who founded them, and the dedication to St Mary of the original Glastonbury church was therefore significant. From this and other clues which he found suggestive, Lionel Lewis persuaded himself that the Virgin Mary had been buried at Glastonbury. The actual spot was marked by a stone, still to be seen low down in the south wall of the St Mary chapel, inscribed in archaic letters, JESU MARIA. That spot, he felt, was hallowed ground. It was the spot referred to in that strangest item of Glastonbury lore, the ancient and garbled Prophecy of

81

Melkin (fully set out in Chapter 16), as the burial place of St Joseph. "He lies", says Melkin, "on a forked line (*linea bifurcata*) next to the southern corner of the oratory made of wattles, over the powerful and adorable virgin." From this Lewis concluded that, after burying the Virgin Mary at Glastonbury, St Joseph himself had been buried in a grave above her. In the St Katherine chapel of his own church, St John's, Lewis believed that he had discovered the ancient tomb of St Joseph, carved with his initials, J.A. (Joseph of Arimathea).

"There is a disease which attacks most scholars who deal with the history of Glastonbury Abbey, a kind of galloping gullibility." So writes James Carley, the Glastonbury historian. He himself has felt "early symptoms of this malady", and he is a leader of the modern tendency among scholars to look kindly upon the Glastonbury legends and to allow them a more genuine antiquity than was previously admitted. What he calls 'gullibility' could perhaps be something deeper and more subtle. It is acknowledged that Glastonbury has power to attract and generate legends. Moreover, those who ponder them, even from a sceptical viewpoint, are likely to fall under their spell; and thereupon they are led into certain channels of thought, familiar to many before them, towards the inner chambers of the Glastonbury mystery.

It is unlikely that we shall ever know the precise details of how the first church was established at Glastonbury. Local history does not reach back that far, and the foundation legends have always been subject to the same process of expansion and elaboration as goes on today. Yet the antiquity and the high significance of the legends is beyond dispute. This is admitted, even by writers who deny the historical basis of all the legends in their present form. As stated by one such critic, R.F. Treharne, author of *The Glastonbury Legends*, the basic fact is that :

> "When the English arrived at Glastonbury soon after 658 they found a great and famous Celtic monastery already established and flourishing there, a monastery already venerated as the holiest place in Britain, with a primacy in time springing from great antiquity stretching back to a lost origin before firm history begins in this part of the land."

Even if it could be proved that Joseph of Arimathea, St Mary or Christ himself visited the Isle of Avalon, even such a remarkable fact would not explain the mystery of Glastonbury, nor would it dispel it. Like the Christian romances of King Arthur and the Grail, the story of St Joseph echoes an earlier, pagan theme. We examine the Glastonbury legends, not in the hope of establishing literal and historical facts, but because they provide the outer keys to the ancient secret of Avalon.

The Christian Revelation

Chapter Ten
Joseph of Arimathea and the
Ancient Wooden Hut

By the twelfth century Glastonbury had accumulated a fabulous collection of treasures and sacred relics, but its most precious object was a simple rustic hut made of wooden stakes and twigs, a circular wattle structure like the huts of Glastonbury's old lake villages. Not much of it was left after a thousand years. Its original timbers, if they still existed at all, had been reduced to a few sticks above the ring of stones at its foundations, but the site was lovingly preserved within a reliquary consisting of a small, rectangular church dedicated to the Virgin Mary. This church itself was venerated as an ancient relic, and in about 625 Paulinus, the first Catholic archbishop of York, caused its wooden walls to be protected by a casing of boards coated with lead. In the sanctuary at the east end of the church were the foundations of the old wattle hut. Pilgrims to Glastonbury, it is supposed, filed through the chapel by doors in its north and south walls, and were allowed to peep into the sanctuary through a gap in the screen which covered a narrow archway.

They glimpsed into a mystic cavern, richly adorned with veils and tapestries, jewelled relics, images and gold crosses, which were made dimly visible through incense fumes by the flames of candles and oil lamps. Many great and holy people were entombed there, including St Patrick of Ireland and St David, patron saint of the Welsh, whose miraculous altar in the form of a great sapphire was one of Glastonbury's treasures. Yet the greatest attraction to pilgrims was the ancient wooden

church, for it bore witness to the truth of Glastonbury's marvellous legend. From that legend had grown the enormous Abbey church to the east of St Mary's. It was the oldest, richest and most famous religious house in England, and the source of its power and holiness lay within the wooden rectangle, the '*vetusta ecclesia*' of the old chroniclers, which the Saxons called simply Ealde Chirche, the Old Church.

The holiness which emanated from the Old Church made a deep impression on the first known historian of Glastonbury, the monkish chronicler William of Malmesbury. He went to Glastonbury in about 1129 at the invitation of the Abbot, Henry of Blois, who wanted him to sort through the ancient documents in the Abbey library and to write up the Lives of famous Glastonbury saints. One result of William's visit was his *De Antiquitate Glastonie Ecclesie* (*The Ancient History of the Church at Glastonbury*), dedicated to Abbot Henry. In it he wrote in terms of awe about the powerful atmosphere generated by the wooden church.

> "From the beginning it was redolent of divine sanctity and spread an air of great reverence throughout the entire country, even despite its uncouth appearance. All the roads to it were therefore crowded with pilgrims; rich men came there having laid aside their wealth, and it was much visited by people of religion and learning.

> "The church at Glastonbury is thus the oldest that I know in England, and thus it has deserved its name, the Old Church. In it... are preserved the bodies of many saints, nor is there any part of the sanctuary where there

are not ashes of the blessed. Not only the stone-paved floor and the sides of the altar, but the very altar itself both above and within, are crammed full of holy relics. That repository of so many saints is justly called a heavenly sanctuary on earth."

This is followed by a tantalizing reference to a "sacred mystery" symbolized by a pattern of inlaid stones on the floor of the Old Church— a subject which recurs in Chapter 15. William then goes on to describe the customs and taboos, appropriate to an ancient pagan sanctuary, which were observed in Glastonbury's precinct.

"Its antiquity and the congregation of its saints have created such reverence for the place that at night scarcely anyone dares to keep vigil there, nor to spit there during the daytime. May whoever is conscious of pollution tremble through his whole body. No one ever brought a horse or a hawk into the neighbouring cemetery and left again without suffering harm to himself or his possessions. Everyone within living memory (with one exception) who has undergone trial by iron or water and offered a prayer there has rejoiced in his salvation. Whenever it has been planned to erect a building nearby, overshadowing the church and blocking its light, that building has fallen into ruin. Certainly to the people of that province there was no more sacred or popular oath than to swear by the Old Church; they would do anything rather than to commit perjury upon that oath, fearing sudden retribution. If the truth of what we have said be doubted, there is evidence from many of the most reliable men down the ages in support of it."

On 25 May 1184 one of the hangings in the Old Church caught fire from a taper, and within minutes the whole building, stuffed with dry old relics, was an inferno. The flames spread to consume most of the

Abbey, including its precious library, but the greatest disaster was the loss of the Old Church itself, not a stick of which survived.

The sanctity which the lost wooden church had instilled throughout the entire country was bound up with its marvellous foundation legend. There were several versions of the legend, varying in detail but all agreeing that the church at Glastonbury was the first and oldest in Britain. The earliest accounts emphasized its divine origin; it was built by God and consecrated by Christ himself. The more rational story, as told to pilgrims by the Abbey guides, was that St Joseph and his followers from the Holy Land had been inspired by the archangel Gabriel to erect the church on that spot.

Before William of Malmesbury went to Glastonbury he was probably aware of this legend in its various forms, but he set no historical value on it. In an earlier book, *De Gestis Pontificum*, he had attributed the foundation of the Abbey to the Saxon King Ine in about 700. The records and relics he discovered at Glastonbury convinced him that the Old Church long predated the Saxon invasion. No doubt he inspected the fragment of wattlework still surviving in his day, and he observed the mystical pattern of mosaic on the church floor, but more impressive to his scholarly mind were the ancient manuscripts in the muniments chamber of the Abbey.

It is unlikely that the Glastonbury library had been catalogued at that time, for the affairs of the Abbey were in a state of disorder. The sixty years following the Norman invasion had been a period of almost constant turmoil. William the Conqueror had appointed a Norman abbot, Thurstan, who pulled down and replaced the old Saxon church of King Ine, and further alienated the monks by introducing a new form of liturgy in place of their old Gregorian chant. Their monks rebelled, and their abbot called in armed men who sacrilegiously massacred some of them before the altar. Thurstan was disgraced and sent back to Normandy.

His successor, Abbot Herluin, demolished Thurstan's church on the grounds that it was not magnificent enough and built another which he considered more worthy of Glastonbury's reputation. These upheavals had disrupted the monastic life. When, in 1126, Henry of Blois, a nephew of King Henry I, became Abbot of Glastonbury, he found the

Two versions of antiquarian imagination on the appearance of the Old Church at Glastonbury.

monastery impoverished and demoralized. One of the steps he took towards restoring the fame and fortune of the Abbey was to persuade William of Malmesbury, the most reputable scholar in the kingdom, to undertake the writing of its history.

The historian was amazed by the antiquity of Glastonbury's records. Its charters went back to before Saxon times, beginning in 601 when a king of Dumnonia (Cornwall, Devon and part of Somerset) granted lands to an ancient British Abbot of Glastonbury. There were fragments of even older documents and references to others long perished. Conditions in the Glastonbury library at that time can be pictured from William's account of how, while he was writing his *Life of St Dunstan*, the monks produced some relevant archives which they had just found in a "very old chest".

In the original version of his history William was able to quote written testimony to the existence of a church at Glastonbury as early as the second century. It was built by two missionaries whom Pope Eleutherius had sent to Britain at the behest of King Lucius. Yet he also found references to an earlier foundation. Certain old British historians had stated that "No other men's hands made the church at Glastonbury, but the very disciples of Christ built it".

One of William's sources, an unnamed book by an ancient British chronicler, was known to the Glastonbury monks, and in a later copy of William's manuscript the relevant passage was quoted more fully.

> "In the western confines of Britain there is a certain royal island, known by its ancient name, Glastonia; it is broad and hilly, surrounded by slow-flowing rivers full of fish, well adapted to supply many human needs and, above all, dedicated to sacred services. There the first English converts to the Christian law discovered, by God's guidance, an ancient church, built, so they say, by no human art but designed by God himself for the salvation of humanity; after which the Maker of Heaven showed by many miracles and mysteries that he had consecrated it to himself and to Mary, the holy mother of God."

This is the esoteric version of the foundation legend, and in fact it gives no support to the more rational account which William found appropriate to the factual tone of his history. After William's death, and particularly after the fire of 1184, the story of twelve disciples, led by Joseph of Arimathea whose name was probably not mentioned in William's original text, became increasingly emphasized in the official Abbey history. The monks regarded themselves as the owner's of William's copyright, and over the years they updated and added new material to his history of Glastonbury. The work survives only in manuscripts which incorporate the thirteenth-century additions, but many passages are authenticated by the fact that William repeated them when he revised one of his previous histories, *De Gestis Rerum Anglorum* (*The Deeds of the Kings of England*).

Comparing the original with the expanded version of William's *De Antiquitate Glastonie Ecclesie*, one can see how Glastonbury's foundation legend was made more literal and historical to the neglect of its mystical aspect. By a corresponding process, the spiritual character of the Abbey had changed by the end of the twelfth century. The loss of the Old Church had deprived Glastonbury of its Celtic inheritance and diminished its atmosphere of mystery. Its new attraction was to Arthurian pilgrims, for a few years after the fire the body of King Arthur was discovered in the Abbey cemetery. Glastonbury became his national shrine, and local saints with Arthurian connections rose to new fame. The most important of those saints was Joseph of Arimathea. He was reputed to have been a kinsman of Sir Galahad and one of King Arthur's forebears.

The story of St Joseph at Glastonbury, as told in the expanded, thirteenth-century version of William of Malmesbury's history, begins with the old tradition that, after the Crucifixion, the Twelve Apostles divided up the world between them, each taking one region as their mission field. To St Philip was allotted Gaul, and by him were sent the first Christian missionaries to Britain.

"He appointed as their leader, so it is said, his dearest friend, Joseph of Arimathea, he who had buried Our Lord. Arriving in Britain in 63 A.D., the fifteenth year after the assumption of the Blessed Mary, they duly preached the faith of Christ. The barbarian king and his people, hearing this preaching which was new and unfamiliar to them, refused to accept it, nor were they willing to change the traditional doctrines of their forefathers. Yet because the missionaries had come from far away, and because their modesty demanded it, the king granted them a certain island in an outlying part of his territory, surrounded by woods, brambles and marshes and known to its inhabitants as Yniswitrin, as a place for their habitation. Later on, two other kings, who, though they themselves were pagans, had heard of the sanctity of their lives, successively bestowed and confirmed upon each of them a portion of land. Thence, it is believed, the Twelve Hides derive the name by which they are still known. Having lived in that wilderness for a short time, the saints were admonished by a vision of the archangel Gabriel to build a church in honour of the holy mother of God, the Virgin Mary, on a place shown to them by heaven. They did not hesitate in obeying this divine order, and they completed the chapel as they had been instructed, making its walls below of withies twisted round in a circle (*per circuitum*), in the thirty-first year after the passion of Our Lord and the fifteenth after the assumption of the glorious Virgin—a somewhat uncouth design no doubt, but adorned by God with many virtues. And since it was the first in that region, the Son of God distinguished it by a greater dignity by dedicating it in honour of his mother. In that same place the twelve saints, showing devoted obedience to God and the blessed Virgin with vigils, fastings and prayers, were provided with all necessities by the Virgin's aid and by a vision of her, so it is believed by the pious."

This account is almost dryly historical. Apart from the traditional reference to the dedication of the church by the Son of God himself, it contains nothing miraculous. Notably absent is any mention of the holy Grail. Yet at the time when William's history was written, St Joseph and the Holy Grail were linked together in Glastonbury's legends. These legends were given literary form in the French Grail romances, poetic compositions designed to express the mystical ideals of Christian chivalry. Robert de Borron in about 1200 told how St Joseph obtained the chalice used at the Last Supper and caught in it some drops of blood from Jesus on the Cross. Inspired by a vision, he and his party travelled to Britain and eventually to the Vale of Avalon, bearing the precious relic which was called the Holy Grail.

On his way to Avalon St Joseph performed a ritual re-enactment of the Last Supper. Upon a table he set the Grail together with a fish which had been caught by his brother-in-law, Brons. Thenceforth Brons was known as the Rich Fisher, and in other romances he played the part of the Fisher King whose mysterious wound had caused the disenchantment of the country. He and his realm could only be healed through the achievement of the Grail Quest and this was finally accomplished by his grandson, Perceval.

This Brons was none other than the old British king, Bran, the possessor of a magical cauldron, a pre-Christian Grail vessel. His association with Glastonbury goes back to even earlier times when, as the British Saturnus or Kronos, he inhabited the Blessed Isles, represented in symbolic geography by the isles of Avalon. Bran, it has been suggested, was the name of Glastonbury's giant spirit guardian during the Age of Taurus. Bran the Blessed was named in one of the old Welsh Triads as the Grail bearer, who first brought Christianity to Wales. His legend thus merged with that of St Joseph.

The medieval Grail romances were gracefully adapted to the age of Christianity, but their contents were derived almost entirely from the ancient British bardic tradition, with themes, names and symbols, such as the Grail and its Guardian, which originated in the pagan Mysteries. This was demonstrated with great clarity by Jessie Weston in 1920. Summarizing the conclusions reached in her book, *From Ritual to Romance*, she wrote:

> " The Grail story is not *du fond en comble* the product of imagination, literary or popular. At its root lies the record, more or less distorted, of an ancient Ritual, having for its ultimate object the initiation into the secret of the sources of Life, physical and spiritual… In its esoteric 'Mystery' form it was freely utilized for imparting of high spiritual teaching concerning the relation of Man to the Divine Source of his being, and the possibility of a sensible union between Man, and God. The recognition of the cosmic activities of the Logos appears to have been a characteristic feature of this teaching, and when Christianity came upon the scene it did not hesitate to utilize the already existing medium of instruction, but boldly identified the Deity of Vegetation, regarded as Life Principle, with the God of the Christian Faith."

By 1342, when Glastonbury's historian monk, John, compiled his *Chronicle,* St Joseph's association with the Grail had become acknowledged in Glastonbury's official history as promulgated at the Abbey. According to John's account, Joseph carried to Britain a pair of 'cruets' containing the blood and sweat of Jesus. These vessels can be seen depicted in a fifteenth-century stained glass portrait of St Joseph in the church at Langport.

The traditional arms of St. Joseph, adopted by the medieval abbots of Glastonbury. The 'rugged cross' refers to St. Joseph's thorn tree, and the vessels are the two cruets he brought from the Holy Land. The descending droplets are the blood and sweat of Jesus, contained in the cruets. They are also suggestive of the alchemical 'heavenly dew', which is a symbol of the prophesied restoration of Glastonbury as a model of paradise on earth.

Another piece of stained glass from the same period, in St John's church at Glastonbury, shows the two cruets emblazoned on the arms of St Joseph. Between them is a green cross made of sprouting thorn twigs. The allusion is to the famous episode in St Joseph's legend when, upon reaching the Isle of Avalon, he thrust his staff into the ground on Wearyall Hill. It took root and grew into the holy thorn tree, which lived on at Glastonbury, blossoming at Christmastide every year up to the seventeenth century, when it fell victim to a Puritan's axe.

The old thorn tree, whose descendant stands today on Wearyall Hill, provides solid evidence for those who like to believe that Joseph of Arimathea actually came to Glastonbury.

On Wearyall Hill stands the successor to St. Joseph's fabulous thorn tree, which blossoms on Christmas Eve.

Nor should they be discouraged by certain disagreeable writers who have asserted that the name of St Joseph was unknown at Glastonbury before he was arbitrarily written into the history of the Abbey by unscrupulous medieval monks. It is unimaginable that a newly-manufactured story would have been accepted by learned scholars and local Somerset people alike. St Joseph's cult at Glastonbury could only have arisen out of a long-standing tradition. There is no doubt that some very important event took place at Glastonbury at the beginning of the Christian era, and that some awesomely holy person was present on that occasion. West Country folklore from Cornwall to Somerset, as summarized in the preceding chapter, firmly identifies that person as Joseph of Arimathea.

Yet, true or not, the simple story of St Joseph is also an allegory, both concealing and hinting at the greater mystery of Glastonbury. Behind the Christian foundation legend lies another, more ancient. It is well known that many of the legends which became attached to Christian saints and sanctuaries were of earlier, pagan origin. Glastonbury's legend is an obvious example, for there is no doubt that Glastonbury was a centre of the ritual Grail cycle in times before Christianity. The adoption by Christianity of the traditional foundation legend at Glastonbury has a special significance; it indicates that the early Church inherited the secrets of the Celtic Mysteries which were symbolized by the twelve zodiacal signs and allegorized in the story of twelve saintly founders.

Like all sacred allegories, the Glastonbury legend has different levels of meaning and has been expressed accordingly in different forms. For children and simple good souls, who like religious history to be credible and personalized, St Joseph and his companions provide a pleasant and likely parable. The early and medieval chroniclers, however, who were writing for the learned few among their contemporaries, approached more nearly to the heart of the mystery when they stated that the Old Church at Glastonbury was not built by any human hands but was created and consecrated by divine power.

Chapter Eleven
Twelve saints and the
Mysterious Conversion of the Celts

The early history of Glastonbury's Old Church, after its mysterious foundation, consists mainly of its successive restorations. When the twelve saints of St Joseph's party died, the site of their settlement reverted to wilderness and the wattle hut stood ruined and neglected. Its discovery and reconsecration in the second century, by the two missionaries sent by Pope Eleutherius, was recorded by William of Malmesbury from "reliable annals" he found in the Glastonbury library. His account was expanded after his death, the names of the two missionaries were discovered, and the thirteenth-century version of William's *Ancient History* contains the following description of how the Old Church was founded anew.

> "There came thus to Britain missionaries of Eleuth-
> erius, two most holy men, the preachers Phagan and
> Deruvian, as is testified to by St Patrick's Charter and
> the Deeds of the Britons. Proclaiming the word of life,
> they baptized the king and his people at the sacred font
> in the year of Our Lord 166. Thus preaching and
> baptizing while travelling through the land of Britain,
> they came, like Moses the law-giver, penetrating into
> the heart of the wilderness, to the isle of Avalon, where
> by God's guidance they found the Old Church which

had been built by the hands of Christ's disciples and prepared by God for the salvation of humanity. Sometime later, the Maker of Heaven himself showed by many miracles and sacred mysteries that he had consecrated it to himself and to Mary, the holy mother of God. The interval between the coming to Britain of the disciples of St Philip and the coming of these saints was 103 years. Thus when the afore-mentioned Saints Phagan and Deruvian discovered that oratory they were filled with ineffable joy and, praising God, they prolonged their sojourn there, for nine years indeed. Upon making a careful investigation of the spot they found a figure of our Redeemer together with other manifest signs by which they clearly understood that Christians had previously occupied the place. It was later made known to them by a heavenly oracle that the Lord had specially chosen that place before all others in Britain for the invocation of the name of his glorious Mother."

The story continues with the discovery by Phagan and Deruvian of some old documents which told them about the previous foundation by the twelve missionaries sent by St Philip. They therefore renewed the original settlement in the same spot and, following the same pattern, chose twelve of their companions to dwell as anchorites in place of the first twelve. Their place of worship was the Old Church which they restored, adding to it a stone-built oratory in honour of Christ and Saints Peter and Paul. King Lucian confirmed in perpetuity the grant of land made by the pagan kings before him, and a succession of holy anchorites continued for many generations to inhabit the spot, always in a group of twelve.

The next recorded episode in Glastonbury's history was the arrival there of Saint Patrick in the fifth century. According to William of Malmesbury's original text, he returned to Britain in his old age, having accomplished the conversion of Ireland. Like several other Celtic saints, he possessed a wonderful altar on which he navigated to Cornwall, and

A carving on the west front of the church tower on Glastonbury Tor shows the Archangel Michael disputing with the Devil over a pair of scales. The Christian archangel inherited two contrasting functions from the Apollonian deity whom he replaced as guardian of the high places. In one aspect he was a solar hero, a champion of light and reason against the powers of darkness. As leader of the heavenly hosts, he was naturally the patron saint of sacred hilltops, but he also had power over the underworld, whose entrance was through caverns beneath his hills. With his scales he weighed the souls of the dead and emphasised their virtues over their vices. He was also the initiator, leading souls through the subterranean ordeals of the Mysteries. Glastonbury Tor is a prominent landmark, a link between heaven and earth and an ancient centre of initiation. Its attributes are thus in perfect correspondence with those of its spiritual ruler, St. Michael.

from there he wandered up to Glastonbury. The successors to the twelve missionary saints were still living there in the original style, in hermit cells around the Old Church. St Patrick reorganized their community, persuading them to live together in a monastery and becoming their first abbot. In St Patrick's charter, compiled in the thirteenth century from traditional Abbey lore and quoted in John of Glastonbury's *Chronicle*, Patrick is said to have climbed the Tor and to have discovered there a ruined oratory to St Michael, together with old records from the time of Saints Phagan and Deruvian.

Another ancient legend, of how Glastonbury came to be populated, was recorded by William of Malmesbury. It is a strange, archaic story about twelve brothers from the north who took possession of four territories in Wales. Their names were Ludnerth, Morgen, Catgur, Cathmor, Merguid, Morvined, Morehel, Morcant, Boten, Morgent, Mortineil and Glasteing. The last of these, Glasteing, followed a wandering sow as far as Wells and then further, along the Sugewege (Sow's Way) to Glastonbury. He found her suckling piglets under an apple tree near the Old Church. Thenceforth apples from that tree were called Old Church apples and the sow was known as the Old Church sow. She was remarkable because, whereas all other sows have four feet, this one had eight. Glasteing was attracted by Glastonbury and brought his family there, who multiplied and populated the entire district. William's authority for this story was the old British historian, Nennius.

In all these stories of Glastonbury's foundation or refoundation the one common factor is the number twelve. First there was the wattle church, said to have been founded by twelve disciples of Christ to whom the British king granted twelve hides of land. Then came the two missionaries from Rome who settled twelve of their followers around the old oratory. Their successors kept up the tradition, always maintaining the number twelve, up to the fifth century when St Patrick reformed them as a monastic twelve with himself as their thirteenth member and leader.

The theme of twelve recurs in the story of Glasteing as one of twelve brothers, and also in the traditional history of St David at Glastonbury. St David went there after the death of St Patrick, intending to found and dedicate a new church. He was warned by Jesus in a dream that he himself had already dedicated the church at Glastonbury to his own mother, so David was content with building an eastward extension to the Old Church. His medieval biographer nevertheless claimed Glastonbury as the first of St David's twelve foundations.

As previously shown in Chapter Seven, the number twelve is a symbol of that traditional form of civilization which was established in all ancient Celtic territories and has flourished at different times and places throughout the world. It was based on a solar calendar with twelve months to the year and twelve gods who each governed one of the twelve zodiacal signs. Its ruling institution was a sacred king, representing the sun. At first he was one of the twelve chiefs in a twelve-tribe confederacy, but his function was later bestowed upon a permanent thirteenth presiding over a council of twelve regional kings. The sacred state myth which accompanied this form of society was, in Celtic countries, the solar epic of King Arthur and his twelve knights.

Each nation of twelve tribes had its own foundation myth, deriving its origins from twelve ancient gods or heroes. Thus the twelve tribes of Israel were descended from twelve brothers, divided into four groups of three, as also were the twelve tribes of the four territories of Wales, who sprang from the twelve brothers in the story of Glasteing. According to Plato, the twelve-tribe states of ancient Greece reflected the former division of the world between the twelve gods, and the twelve members of the ruling councils of those states represented the twelve local deities from whom they had received their law. The coming to Britain of Brutus the Trojan, advised by a council of twelve elders, typifies the foundation myth of the Celtic civilization in Britain.

The early Christian councils and missionary groups of twelve members were ostensibly modelled on Christ and the twelve apostles. Yet that model was itself derived from earlier prototypes. In the monasteries of the Jewish Essene sect, whose mystical doctrines were thought to have been assimilated by Jesus through John the Baptist, all institutions were organized on a basis of twelve. St John in Revelation followed the Essene tradition with his depiction of the New Jerusalem as a city with twelve gates, corresponding to the twelve tribes of Israel and to other twelve-fold systems. His visionary city, like Plato's twelve-tribe city-state of Magnesia, was an image of the traditional cosmology, the numerically codified model of God's creation which has inspired all the examples of twelve-tribe, zodiacally ordered nations throughout history. In Jewish mysticism, the regathering of Israel's twelve tribes at Jerusalem is the essential prelude to the restoration of divine government, as in the days of King Solomon. Jesus's mission was entirely to his own Jewish people, his intention being to make them worthy of their twelve-tribe inheritance and thus to expedite the Millenium. By choosing twelve followers he symbolized that aim in the conventional manner, for according to one of nature's underlying laws, demonstrated through arithmetic, mystical and magical operations are most effectively worked by groups of twelve, as in a coven of witches. Our custom of twelve men to a jury commemorates the ancient assemblies of twelve law-givers, symbolizing the twelve astrological signs and types of human nature.

Mystical idealists and revivalists are traditionally organized in twelves, for that number is the emblem of the sacred order which they seek to restore. Thus Odysseus led twelve heroes, there were twelve Arthurian knights and Charlemagne's court was composed of his twelve nobles. The Scandinavian berserker knights fought in bands of twelve in imitation of Odin's twelve-god pantheon, and in the royal courts of ancient Ireland twelve chosen warriors formed the entourage of the king.

Jesus and the twelve apostles are but one example of a pattern which was well established in their time and has frequently arisen since. It was not merely Christian piety which caused the Order of Knights Templar at Jerusalem to elect their Grand Master through a twelve-member college, allot him twelve servants, appoint twelve knights as elite guardians of the True Cross and conduct twelve-part initiation ceremonies adapted from the pagan Mysteries, wherein the candidate had to undergo twelve ordeals, three by each of the four elements. The Christian symbolism in these rites was merely superficial, for the secret knowledge and science professed by the Templars came from a far earlier tradition. Similarly, the legend of twelve missionary founders, which occurs throughout Christendom but particularly in Celtic countries, was an item of pagan mythology which Christianity renewed.

This transference from pagan to Christian religion of mystical lore and number symbolism is in accordance with what Celtic scholars have long asserted, that the laws, rites and doctrines of the early Celtic Church were basically the same as those of the Celtic Druids. Celtic Christianity has indeed been called a mere reformation of Druidry. A unique and remarkable feature of the early Church in Britain and Ireland is that it claimed no martyrs through persecution by the religion it supplanted. Its proto-martyr was St Alban at the end of the third century, whom the Romans beheaded. It is generally agreed that, for the most part, the Druids had no difficulty in accepting the new religion, because it scarcely interfered with the existing religious and social order. The system of the early Church, writes J. Willis Bund in *The Celtic Church of Wales*, "was really Paganism with a veneer of Christianity".

The conversion of Britain was clearly not achieved by popular preaching. Even in areas such as Glastonbury, where the influence of the Druids had been weakened by the Roman occupation and commerce, the tribal system was still in force, and the religion of each tribe was determined by the chief and his hierarchy. The procedure of the first Christian missionaries, it appears, was to persuade tribal chiefs as to the advantages of Christianity. If they and their advisers were won over, their people followed them in converting to the new faith. Each tribe had its religious precinct with its sacred grove, memorials and place of initiation, and at the more important centres were the Druid monastic colleges. Upon the conversion of a tribe, its Druid sanctuary became the first site of a Christian settlement, known in Wales as the 'tribe of the saint'. Since all the members of a tribe, including their learned men and priests, were normally related to each other as a clan, it was quite natural that the local Druids and their pupils should retain their previous functions under Christianity. Many a saint of the early Church began his career in one of the Druid colleges.

The great mystery behind early Christianity in Britain is how the first missionaries managed to persuade the chiefs, nobles and Druids, the established hierarchy of highly traditional societies, to lead their people in converting to the new faith of Christ. Certainly there was opposition, referred to in several of the early saints' legends, but there is no record of violence and bloodshed. Contests between the rival men of religion, Druid and Christian, took place on a professional level, as trials between rival magicians. We only hear, of course, about those engagements where Christians won, but it appears that their magic was generally superior to that of their opponents. Thus St Patrick prevailed over the Druids of Tara, St Columba defeated the Druids of Bruidh and St David won a contest with the magician Boia. In times when the outcomes of battles were largely determined by the powers of the Druids on each side, a compelling inducement to accept Christianity was that Christian magic proved more effective than that of the pagans.

Here we are on unfamiliar ground, for the arts of ancient magical warfare are no longer known and it is impossible to say by what combinations of psychology, conjuring, weather control and elemental invocation prehistoric battles were conducted. It is clear, however, that the magic of tribal shamans is ineffectual against outsiders of a different religion. The ultimate triumph of Christ, the Light of the World, over the darker magic of the Druids was similar in many ways to the victory, some two thousand years earlier, of the light-bearing heroes of the Celtic, Bronze Age civilization against the earth powers of the megalithic magicians.

A deeper cause behind the success of Christianity can be seen in the traditional method of astrological time reckoning known throughout the ancient world. Modern historians have generally felt themselves unqualified to deal with this subject, and the influence of astrological ages has scarcely been acknowledged. Yet there is no doubt that the Druid priests at the beginning of the Christian era would have been well aware that the old age of Aries was giving way to that of Pisces, and they would therefore have been alert to portents of psychic changes which, according to ancient Egyptian records, occur during such periods of transition.

The due revelation which the Druids awaited, for which their sacred prophecies were likely to have prepared them, came in the form of Christianity. The tidings of Christ's Crucifixion and of the mystical Salvation thereby promised, quickly reached Britain, brought directly from the Holy Land. Thus the rites and customs of the Celtic Church were of an eastern, Orthodox character, quite different from those of Rome. The Celts were unique in their spirituality, both before and after they adopted Christianity. Together with their theology, many of their old gods passed into the new religion as Christian saints and archangels. St Michael, guardian of Glastonbury Tor and other ancient high places, assumed the role of the Celtic Apollo. By the sixth century, Celtic and Anglo-Saxon missionaries from monasteries in Britain and Ireland were spreading the worship of angels throughout Europe, thus spiritualizing the Roman form of Christianity which was then based on ancestor-worship of local saints.

As King Arthur's Round Table consisted of twelve knights, so the Celtic missionaries travelled and preached in groups of twelve.

Not only Glastonbury but many other regions in the British Isles and beyond claim a tradition of having received Christianity through a company of twelve saints. Scotland, Wales and Cornwall are all said to have been evangelized by such a group. The earliest of these legends comes from South Wales, where the foundation of the old Celtic sanctuary at Llantwit Major is attributed to St Ilid in the year 56. Like Joseph of Arimathea he was a Jew from the Holy Land, and he also came to Britain in a party of twelve. His royal patroness was St Eurgain, the wife of Caractacus who fought against the Romans. The twelve saints of St Ilid dwelt as anchorites around an oratory. Their community developed in the same way as Glastonbury's, being reformed on monastic lines early in the sixth century by the learned St Illtyd. Thereafter, the college at Llantwit Major became one of the greatest centres of education in Europe.

According to the Life of Cornwall's patron saint, St Petroc, he purified the West Country by expelling a foul monster which had devastated the land. With twelve companions he established a community of hermits on Bodmin Moor, and so powerful was their influence that the wild moorlands became fertile and populous.

Another sixth-century missionary saint with twelve companions was St Paul, a Briton who was educated at St Illtyd's college in Llantwit Major. He also went to Cornwall, to the court of King Mark, and thence proceeded to Brittany where he and his twelve saints founded a number of churches.

From the Scottish island sanctuary of Iona came several recorded groups of twelve missionaries. Iona itself was founded by twelve saints, led by St Columba, and the missions it sponsored included that of St Aidan who chose twelve boys from his monastery at Lindisfarne to be his apostles in the evangelizing of Northumbria. In their missions to the Continent the Celtic saints maintained the tradition of founding churches in parties of twelve. The most famous of these, St Columban, settled with twelve companions in Gaul, and his disciple St Gall was also one of twelve when he brought Celtic Christianity to Switzerland. Emphasized in all these legends are the benefits which the twelve saints bestowed on the localities where they settled. Through their sanctifying influence deserts flowered and countrysides grew prosperous. The feeling conveyed in many local accounts of the twelve saints is that, wherever they sojourned, the Grail was temporarily restored to earth.

Most of these stories are drawn from the Lives of Celtic saints, and they are properly called legends because the Lives were written long after the deaths of their subjects, by medieval monks who wished to encourage local saintly cults. Yet it was certainly the custom of the Celtic Christians to evangelize and to found churches in units of twelve. The practice seems to have been that, first, a ritual foundation ceremony was performed by twelve holy men in a former pagan sanctuary. The twelve lived in hermits' cells around an oratory, where they maintained in turn a ceaseless round of prayers and chants. Around them grew a community of their pupils and followers (the 'tribe of the saint'). In the course of time, twelve of their initiates, instructed in the priestly, geomantic and astrological arts of church-foundation, were sent out to plant a new Christian community within another tribe.

This procedure was so effective that, by the early sixth century in Ireland, the pattern of twelve saints round an oratory had expanded to a national scale, and the whole country was christianized under the Twelve Apostles of Ireland. Among the Apostles were some of the great names in Ireland's sacred history, including St Columba before his mission to Iona and St Brendan the Navigator who was said to have preached in America. Each of them was a head of an important monastery, and their supreme authority was St Finnian of Clonnard in Meath, the Middle County of Ireland.

With this arrangement the Church replicated the hierarchical division of Ireland into twelve tribal kingdoms, three to each of the four provinces, centred on the court of the High King in Meath. Clearly St Finnian took over the religious functions of a former Chief Druid, presiding over a synod of twelve priests. Nor was this pattern limited to Celtic countries. Iceland, where the system of twelve tribes in four provinces was instituted by the early settlers at the beginning of the tenth century, was evangelized a hundred years later by twelve missionaries led by Asolf Alskik. At the opposite end of the Christian world, in Georgia south of the Caucasus mountains, an ancient twelve-tribe union was centred on Pshavi. The conversion of that country, in the fifth century, was effected by the customary twelve missionaries. Known as the Twelve Syrian Fathers, they were followers of St Simeon Stylites who spent much of his life atop a pillar in the Syrian desert. From their first settlement in Georgia they spread across the country, each inhabiting a wilderness and founding a monastery there. Thus the sacred pattern of early Christian Georgia was the same as that of Ireland under St Finnian.

The story of Joseph of Arimathea merges with that of King Arthur at Glastonbury, and the group of twelve is prominent in their combined history. In the Grail romances St Joseph's sister married Bran, the Celtic Grail Keeper, and bore him twelve children. St Joseph is said to have established in Britain the Round Table, guarded by twelve knights of the Order of the Holy Grail. On the same pattern as the Round Table was the twelve-nation kingdom which King Arthur gained through victories in his twelve battles. Reflected in this theme of twelves is the social structure of Celtic civilization, described in Chapter Seven, which was based on the image of the sun passing through the twelve houses of the zodiac. In the *High History of the Holy Grail* the ancient order is allegorized in the story of Alain, one of twelve brother knights who possessed twelve castles, clearly corresponding to the twelve zodiacal signs.

In the light of this universal tradition of twelve saintly founders, springing from an older tradition of the Celtic solar civilization, Glastonbury's foundation legend is no longer seen in isolation and its meaning becomes clearer. St Joseph and his companions bore with them to Glastonbury the secrets of a religious mystery which the Druids had once known but in their period of decadence had lost. Its outward symbol was the cup used at the Last Supper or the two cruets containing relics of Jesus, but more essentially it was the Holy Grail. The Grail is also a symbol, and what it implies is a state of grace, spread over a whole country. Achieving the Grail was a long, disciplined process, an operation of ritual magic requiring constant prayers, chants, fastings and the performance of certain rites of an esoteric and alchemical nature. To perfect this operation, to generate and sustain the golden age atmosphere represented by the Grail, was a full-time task for twelve dedicated initiates.

The techniques of theurgy and ritual magic are mysteries to the uninitiated, but it is safe to say that the most important of the arts which contributed to the Grail ritual was music. In the ancient world, music was both respected and feared because of the effect it has on human temperaments. Plato has much to say about the power of music in its different forms to ennoble minds or debase them. Within the structured, solar societies of antiquity, which Plato wished to restore, the permitted modes of music were specified and upheld by law, disruptive forms being forbidden. The earliest rulers were said to have promulgated their laws entirely through music, and even in times of solar civilization music was still the principal means by which societies were kept both internally harmonious and in tune with the cosmos.

The prescribed music in ancient and Celtic civilizations was heard and performed on every level throughout society, the same mode being adapted to religious chant, bardic ballads, the popular songs at festivals and those sung by children. Music set the tone for the whole country, and in Celtic Britain the Druidic bards were responsible for maintaining its purity, for if the traditional harmonies lost their hold and unlawful music was heard, even at a rustic feast, the religious spell which the Druids cast over their nations would be weakened and ultimately dissolved.

From chanting comes the word enchantment, and it was largely by chanting that the Druids kept up the spell of enchantment which they spread across each of the Celtic kingdoms. It can be assumed, from ancient traditions passed down through the Celtic Church, that a perpetual chant was at one time maintained by the bards of each tribe. The chant was related astrologically to its time and place and progressed through the seasons of the year. It was a twelve-part chant, based on the twelve notes of the chromatic scale, and it was perpetuated by twelve choristers, one for each hour of the day and of the night. Each note corresponded to one of the signs of the zodiac and thus to one of the twelve tribes in a Celtic kingdom. At the twelve great religious centres of each nation, the music of the choirs was based on the note which pertained astrologically to their respective districts. Once a year, when the twelve tribes came together at the national sanctuary, all twelve choirs performed together the complete cycle of their mythological chant.

The most notable feature of the Celtic Church was that it introduced a new liturgical chant and maintained it day and night in every Christian community. At first it was performed by twelve anchorites around a simple oratory, but by the sixth century the power of the chant, combined with other items of Christian priestcraft, had spread its influence over entire countries, and great churchmen such as St David and St Finnian were supreme over a national hierarchy with twelve principal monasteries. Thousands of young monks at each of these centres contributed to its perpetual choir.

One of the perpetual choirs was at Glastonbury. The twelve missionary saints who brought Christianity to Glastonbury were also twelve choristers. Part of the religious secret which they possessed concerned the magical power of music, and the nature of their music can be inferred from a tradition in the Coptic Church, that Christianity prevailed because it inherited arcane musical knowledge and the twelve-part temple chant from the priests of Egypt.

The ancient priestly chant, passed down from the twelve founder saints and traditionally from St Joseph himself, was probably the most cherished possession of Glastonbury Abbey in its earlier days, apart from the wattle church itself. There is no reason for the chant to have changed during the period of Celtic Christianity, and it is known that long after the Celts were suppressed by the Roman Church, the Glastonbury monks maintained, sometimes in secret, many of the ancient rites and practices. Possibly they were still performing the traditional chant of St Joseph at the end of the eleventh century, for when the first Norman abbot, Thurstan, tried to impose a new, Roman chant upon them, their insistence upon retaining their old music was so stubborn that it caused the outrage of 1096 when several recalcitrant monks were slaughtered before the altar.

Chanting was one aspect of the Grail secret, but other mystical sciences made their contributions to the Christian re-enchantment of Britain. At the root of all was that traditional code of cosmology framed by the twelve signs of the zodiac. Now one can see why the Druids and pagan kings accepted the legitimacy of the Christian revelation. In its religious mysteries they recognized the ancient science and doctrines which had been established at the beginning of their civilization, but from which they had long fallen away. Moreover, whenever the Christians were opposed, the power of Christ usually prevailed over pagan magic. Thus the Druids and Christians found common ground in effecting a reformation of Druidry, proclaiming a Celtic Church and practising the religious arts which were designed to procure the restoration of the Grail.

Chapter Twelve
The Wattle Church and the Hall of Light

The original thatched, wood and wattle hut, which formed the central locus of the early Christian mysteries at Glastonbury, has significant parallels in religious traditions elsewhere. Examples of such a building, simple and primitive yet supremely holy, were known in ancient Rome, in China and Japan and, nearer home, at Stonehenge, where archaeologists have found evidence of a circular wooden structure, probably thatched, which was replaced in about 2000 B.C. by the existing ring of sarsen stones. The wooden hut at Stonehenge lies far beyond the reach of history or legend, but other examples have traditional associations which are comparable with those of the Old Church at Glastonbury and thus shed light on its original meaning.

In William Soothill's book, *The Hall of Light*, is a description of the Regia in Rome, the earliest religious building in the Forum and the symbolic centre of Roman state religion. It was round and conical, "built of wattle, with a thatched roof". Known as the Little House of Numa, it was said to have been built and inhabited by the second Roman king after Romulus, Numa Pompilius, at the beginning of the sixth century B.C. He was the founder of the Roman religion and instituted its feasts, sacrifices, sacred calendar and its orders of priests, Vestal virgins and augurs. Near the Regia was a sacred grove where Numa would meet his wife, the nymph Egyria who inspired him with her wisdom.

As the religion of ancient Rome grew more elaborate together with its civilization, the primitive hut was several times restored and rebuilt, but it retained throughout its original form and simplicity. Each successive rebuilding is likely to have preserved the original dimensions of Numa's hut. Under the Republic, the Regia formed the inner sanctum of the Pontifex Maximus, the Roman high priest. The most sacred relics were kept within it, and from its doorway was proclaimed the calendar of religious feasts for the coming year.

Similar to the Regia, both in appearance and function, was the first Chinese temple, the circular, thatched, wooden-walled Ming T'ang, the Hall of Light. The original Ming T'ang was built by Shen Nung, the legendary second emperor of China who is associated with the beginnings of agriculture. The plan he followed had originally been revealed by the first ruler, Fu Hsi, who, in about 2852 B.C., instituted the Chinese system of religion.

In ancient China there were five main examples of the Ming T'ang, one of them below the principal sacred mountain and the other four below the sacred mountains at the four quarters of the kingdom. Others were founded by later rulers near their various capitals. In every case the foundation plan repeated that of Hu Fsi, and every Ming T'ang imitated the primitive character of its ancient prototype. The roof was a cone of untrimmed thatch, and the timbers were plain, undressed oaken boughs. It was located far away from other buildings, in a lonely spot surrounded by water. The robes of its priests and the vessels used in their rituals were coarse and unadorned.

The original Ming T'ang was evidently the sanctum of an astronomer-priest-magician whose position was similar to that of a shamanic Druid among the neolithic tribes of Britain. He observed the stars, the weather and other signs in nature, made contact with the spirit world, placated the gods and pronounced the times and forms of sacrifices. Festooned with bones, relics and other magical accessories, his wooden hut was the holy of holies and the centre of tribal arcana.

In later times the primitive Ming T'ang was overlaid with marble, and state institutions of religion and sacred science grew up around it. Colleges of astronomy and astrology, geomancy and priestcraft were founded in its precinct, and it was the focus of a ceaseless ritual accompanied by music and chant. Yet the primal simplicity of the Ming T'ang itself was always maintained in memory of the founder to whom the secrets of religion were first revealed. Moreover, each new addition

An example of the Ming T'ang in China, built at the foot of a sacred mountain.

to the sacred site was carried out in accordance with a scheme of number and proportion which formed the essence of the original revelation. Thus the great temple complex of later times conformed in its planning to a preordained scheme whose guiding symbol was displayed by the Ming T'ang. That symbol was the 'squared circle', denoting reconciliation between all the opposite elements in nature but especially between heaven and earth. All ancient civilizations were built upon that symbol. The Ming T'ang was therefore round with a conical roof in imitation of the heavenly, spiritual circle, while the platform on which it stood was built as a rational square to represent the earth and the world of matter.

Centred on the squared circle image of the Ming T'ang, a scheme of cosmological geometry determined the form and growth of the Chinese temple precinct. Each of its dimensions, numerically expressed in units of the sacred measures, had a certain significance, and this was acknowledged by Chinese scholars who, long after the transcendental meaning of the Ming T'ang was forgotten, studied its dimensions as intensely as Jewish cabalists study the measurements of the Temple at Jerusalem. Soothill indeed compares the duodecimal number system of the Ming T'ang with the twelve-gated city of St John's New Jerusalem. Both were expressions of a traditional cosmological science, and both were derived from the same traditional model. The New Jerusalem, framed throughout in units of twelve, accommodated the twelve tribes of Israel, while the twelve halls of the developed Ming T'ang diagram corresponded to the twelve administrative divisions of China, instituted by the emperor Yao in the third millenium B.C. Chinese temple music was similarly derived from a scale of twelve semitones. These notes were sounded by twelve bamboo-pipes, each of a different length, and the lengths represented the standard units of measure. Music, measure and architectural proportion were thus combined within a numerical canon based on the number twelve.

Another institution which Soothill compares to the Regia and the Ming T'ang is the primitive wooden hut, constructed without nails, where the Japanese emperor spends a prolonged period in solitary communion with the spirits of his ancestors before his accession to the throne.

Soothill also identifies Stonehenge as a western equivalent to the

Ming T'ang, sharing both its original shape and its astronomical function. This comparison has gained strength with the modern realization that the large post holes, which excavators have discovered on the circumferences of the two outer stone rings at Stonehenge, must originally have supported the timbers of a large wooden hut. Its inner diameter was about 98 feet, and within the outer wall was another, about 80 feet in diameter, whose timbers would have helped to support a thatched roof. An inner circle contained the holy of holies. The geometry of the Stonehenge groundplan shows that, like the Ming T'ang, it formed the symbol of the squared circle.

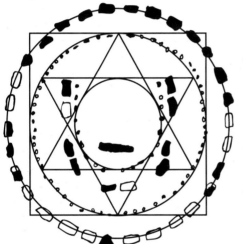

The basic 'squared circle' in the groundplan of Stonehenge. The square, drawn with its perimeter equal in length to the mean circumference of the outer sarsen circle, contains the circle of 'bluestones'. Within this, a six-pointed star contains a circle of the same width as the inner bluestone formation. These proportions echo those of the wooden hut previously on the site.

The archaeologist, Aubrey Burl, who gives the evidence of the former wooden hut in his book, *The Stonehenge People*, likens it to the bone-infested medicine lodge of a tribal shaman. Several of its features were retained in the stone temple which replaced it, including its entrances, one of which was to the south and another to the north-east, where the sun appears at midsummer and the moon rises at the most northerly point of its cycle. Other angles on which the seasonal lights of the sun or moon were allowed to enter the later temple were probably copied from the directions of doors and windows in the original wooden hut.

The earliest works at Stonehenge are dated to around the beginning of the third millenium B.C., and the wooden hut may have stood there until about 2000 B.C. when it was replaced by the rings of stone. It is uncertain whether or not the rings of stone were made to support a roof, but in every other respect the new temple imitated the form of the original hut.

Most carefully preserved were the original dimensions. The inner diameter of the hut was similar to that of the great sarsen circle, 97⅓ feet, and the diameter of its interior wall, about 80 feet, corresponded to that of the Stonehenge bluestone circle. The dimensions of the central sanctum were probably commemorated by the setting of the inner Stonehenge structures around the Altar stone. Thus the astronomically aligned stone temple at Stonehenge perpetuated the shape, measurements and functions of the previous shamanic hut with its wooden walls and thatched roof.

These examples of circular wooden huts as the focus points for great religious systems seem clearly relevant to the mystery of Glastonbury's ancient wattle church. The main characteristics of the Ming T'ang, Regia and other such places was, first, that they were of primeval simplicity, unadorned and built of natural, unworked material. Secondly, they were associated with the founder of the state religion, who had planned them according to a revealed, esoteric code of number. As holy relics they were preserved in their original forms while great temples grew up around them. The third and most significant feature of these wooden huts is that their measurements were held sacred, and every time they were rebuilt or encased within a more permanent structure, their original dimensions were preserved in the new building.

All these features pertained also to Glastonbury's Old Church. Emphasized by the old historians were its utter simplicity and its supreme holiness. It was built under divine guidance by the founders of Christianity in Britain, and it formed the nucleus of England's oldest and greatest Abbey. Above all, the site and shape of the Old Church were always carefully recorded as symbols of a deep religious mystery.

The Ming T'ang and the Regia were places of constant ritual. In and around them a group of initiates worked a religious spell, evidently following a traditional, magical procedure, and thus they founded the

The distillation of heavenly dew, a stage in the alchemical work, pictured by Walter Crane in his frontispiece to The High History of the Holy Grail.

state religions of ancient China and Rome. A similar pattern of events is apparent in Glastonbury. Twelve missionaries, adepts in priestly magic, brought the Christian revelation to Britain. For the site of their operations they chose a spiritually powerful spot, the ancient sanctuary of Avalon. There they fenced off an area and dedicated it to their guide, the spirit of Christ, whose kingdom they sought to establish on earth. Within the fence, which cut them off from the mundane world beyond, they levelled the ground and marked its surface with a combination of geometric figures, following the traditional design. At the centre of the pattern they raised an altar, and upon it they placed a sacred vessel emblematic of the Grail and corresponding to the vessel in which the alchemists performed their great work of redeeming the earth. The altar was enclosed within a circular, wooden oratory.

The twelve priests then began a long-term magical operation, invoking the power of Christ for the restoration of the ancient enchantment of Britain. The lives of those men were dedicated to maintaining a ritualized Grail quest within a sacred precinct specially designed to make their rituals effective. It was, as William of Malmesbury described it, a heavenly sanctuary. Insulated from the outside world, the twelve created a spiritual reality within their circle, and from the wattle church at Glastonbury came a holy light and atmosphere which spread their influence throughout the country.

At the foundation of this sacred work was a cosmological groundplan, a geometric figure expressing certain numbers and measures, which represented the ideal heaven and earth. It was a symbol of the spiritual reality which the twelve holy men experienced among themselves. In the following chapters we examine the Glastonbury foundation plan, for in it are discovered the mystical aspirations of the first Christians and the sacred science by which they conducted their quest for paradise on earth.

Chapter Thirteen
The Foundation Pattern

From the sparse records of Glastonbury's Old Church, its history can be summed up as follows.

A.D. 63 (alternatively 37) is the chronicled date of St Joseph's mission and the building of the wattle church. William of Malmesbury's account implies a tradition that the original building was circular. The twelve missionaries had their cells around it.

In about 166 came a new missionary band led by Saints Phagan and Deruvian. They repaired the wattle church and appointed twelve of their number to continue the rituals of the former twelve.

In 433 St Patrick is said to have become the first abbot of Glastonbury, and to have formed the twelve anchorites into a monastic community. It may have been in St Patrick's time that the round wattle hut was enclosed by a rectangular wooden church.

Early in the sixth century St David visited Glastonbury and claimed it as one of his twelve foundations. He added a building to the east end of the Old Church and, to mark the place where the new works adjoined the old, he caused a pillar to be erected due north of the junction point.

Some time later, according to William of Malmesbury, another church was added by Glasteing, one of the twelve brothers from the north of England.

In 625 or thereafter, Paulinus, a companion of St Augustine, encased the Old Church in wooden boards covered with lead.

In about 725 King Ine of Wessex completed the large stone church dedicated to Saints Peter and Paul to the east of the wooden church. In his charter, which he signed in the wooden church, he confirmed the rights of Glastonbury's seven islands as a perpetual sanctuary. St Dunstan in the middle of the tenth century enlarged Ine's church and added further monastic buildings. Under the early Norman abbots the Saxon church was destroyed and the Abbey was reconstructed on a grander scale.

Throughout all periods, amid all the changes taking place around it, the wooden church remained essentially unaltered. Its ancient timbers sheltered the sacred foundation site until 1184, when the great fire consumed all.

Immediately after the fire the monks began to rebuild the Abbey. Their first concern was to protect the holy ground formerly covered by the Old Church, and within about two years they had completed and dedicated to St Mary a magnificent new stone chapel. It is the same building whose ruins are encountered today as one enters the Abbey grounds. Its walls inside and without were panelled with arcades of intersecting semi-circular arches, giving it a somewhat archaic appearance as if in imitation of its venerable predecessor. With its finely carved stones in a variety of natural colours, vaulted columns supporting its high, hipped roof and tall pinnacled towers at each of its four corners, the new chapel resembled a large, Gothic jewel box. It was in fact a reliquary, a large-scale version of those elaborate caskets which held the venerated bones of kings and saints. After the fire, the monks gathered up the charred fragments of their relics collection, and other saintly bones were exhumed from beneath the floor of the Old Church. These were exhibited in the new chapel to pilgrims who filed past them through the north and south doorways, but the holiest of Glastonbury's relics was its sacred patch of earth, the site of St Joseph's oratory.

At the time of the fire Glastonbury was without a ruler, its abbot having recently died, and King Henry II sent his own chamberlain, Ralph Fitzstephen, to undertake the work of rebuilding. A Glastonbury monk of that time, Adam of Damerham, recorded that Ralph "brought to completion the church of St Mary on the place where the Old Church originally had stood". It was also said that the eastern wall of the new chapel was built over the foundations of the ancient east wall. As originally built, the chapel of St Mary stood detached at the west end of

In the lonely light of midwinter the walls of Glastonbury's St. Mary chapel stand guard over the site of England's first Christian foundation.

the great Abbey Church, but at the end of the thirteenth century its eastern wall was removed, and it was joined to the main church by a new building known as the Galilee. This was probably done to accommodate religious processions between the two churches, but it involved the sacrifice of an important feature of the St Mary chapel. The chapel had been designed to preserve the exact dimensions of the wooden church. When the wall was pulled down to give access to the Galilee, the demarcation line became blurred. It could still, however, be determined by means of a curious monument which stood a few yards away from the Old Church, to the north of its east end.

The monument was a stone pillar, erected in the sixth century when St David built onto the east end of the Old Church. The purpose of the pillar was to mark the north–south line which delimited the eastern extent of St Joseph's church.

Affixed to the pillar was a brass plaque with a Latin text, summarizing the history of the Old Church with special reference to St David, and explaining what the pillar signified. The plaque was added in about 1400, probably in place of an earlier inscription. After the Dissolution it was found among the Abbey ruins, and in the sixteenth century a print, taken directly from it, was published in Spelman's *Concilia*. This was fortunate since the original plaque has since been lost.

Spelman's illustration is reproduced opposite. Its inscription, translated literally (by John Goodall) reads:

> "The 31st year after the Passion of the Lord twelve saints, among whom Joseph of Arimathea was the first, came here. They built in this place that church, the first in this realm, which Christ in honour of his mother, and the place for their burial, presently dedicated. St David, archbishop of Menevia *(i.e., Wales)*, rested here. To whom the Lord (when he was disposed to dedicate that church), appeared in sleep and recalled him from his purpose, also in token that the same Lord had first dedicated that church with the cemetery: He pierced the bishop's hand with his finger, and thus pierced it appeared in the sight of many on the morrow. Afterwards indeed the same bishop as the Lord revealed, and the number of the saints in the same grew: added a chancel to the eastern part of this church and consecrated it in honour of the Blessed Virgin. The altar whereof, of priceless sapphire, he marked the perpetual memory of these things. And lest the site or size of the earlier church should come to be forgotten because of such additions, he erected this column on a line drawn southwest through the two eastern angles of the same church, and cutting it off from the aforesaid chancel. And its length was 60 feet westward from that line, its breadth was truly 26 feet; the distance from the centre of this pillar from the midpoint between the aforesaid angles, 48 feet."

In 1921 during his excavations at the Abbey ruins, Frederick Bligh Bond was asked by his supervisor, Dean Robinson of Wells, to follow

Spelmans's illustration of the plaque from Glastonbury Abbey describing the history of the Old Church (see translation opposite).

up the clues given on the plaque. He dug where the measurements indicated, and at a distance of 48 feet from the centre of St Mary's chapel he uncovered the base of the pillar, resting on a more ancient, circular foundation about seven feet wide. He also discovered the rectangular footings of another monumental structure outside the south porch of the chapel. This he believed to have been one of the two 'pyramids' or pillar crosses between which the tomb of King Arthur and his Queen was excavated in about 1190. The site of this pyramid is shown on Bond's plan. Beside it to the east he marked another, but this was merely conjecture and Bond was never able to investigate the second site.

The monuments whose sites Bond thought he had discovered were the pair of stone cross shafts, described by William of Malmesbury and many writers after him, which were finally pulled down in the eighteenth century. Upon them were inscribed names of early kings and abbots, but the letters became effaced by weathering, and the medieval Glastonbury monks believed them to have recorded the names of the twelve hermits who welcomed St Patrick to Glastonbury. The pillars were known to mark an important burial in the Abbey cemetery. St Joseph of Arimathea was said to lie between them, but when the site was investigated after the great fire, the bones discovered sixteen feet below the surface were identified as those of another distinguished figure in Glastonbury's mythology.

The meaning of this discovery has been argued over ever since. The brisk nineteenth-century view was that the whole excavation was a fake, designed to provide the Abbey with a spurious attraction to pilgrims, their genuine relics having been lost in the fire. Modern archaeology, however, has confirmed that there was indeed an ancient burial at the spot where the monks claimed to have found Arthur and Guinevere. There are several contemporary accounts of the excavation. It was said to have been ordered by King Henry II, who had been informed on the location of Arthur's body by a Welsh bard, and the position of the burial was further indicated by certain miraculous signs. With so much prestige at stake, the monks must have known beforehand that they would find something important; but what they actually found was almost too good to be true. The bones said to be King Arthur's were coffined in a hollowed oak trunk; they were of gigantic size and the skull was pierced

The foundations of St. David's Pillar, exposed during Bligh Bond's excavations, and (below) his plan of how the pillar and the 'pyramids' were placed in relation to St. Mary's Chapel.

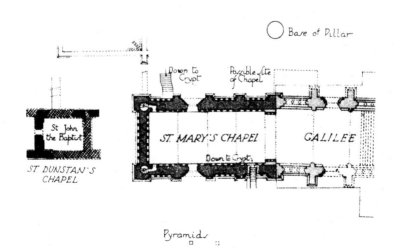

with several wounds, one of which had left a large hole while others had healed up. With Guinevere's skull was found a tress of her golden hair. To put the identification beyond doubt, a leaden cross beneath a stone in the tomb bore a Latin inscription: 'Here lies the famous King Arthur buried in the Isle of Avalon.'

The bones were transferred to the Lady chapel—the chapel of St Mary, newly built after the fire—and in 1278 they were ceremonially enshrined, in the presence of King Edward I and Queen Eleanor, before the high altar of the Abbey church. They vanished at the Dissolution, together with the magnificent tomb of black marble that contained them.

The question of whose bones they actually were is still bitterly disputed, and Glastonbury friendships are still endangered by the controversy. Geoffrey Ashe, whose scholarship in Arthurian matters is beyond rivalry, sees Arthur as a fifth-century British king who fought the invading Saxons and held his court of Camelot at South Cadbury hill. Such a figure is indeed mentioned by the old British chroniclers and fabulists, such as Geoffrey of Monmouth, but his historical status is diluted by the mythological deeds attributed to him. Moreover, the legend of King Arthur goes back to far earlier times than the fifth century, and its geographical expanse is far too wide to be attributed to the fame of a local British ruler. Many ancient kings were buried in the Isle of Avalon, and many of them must have borne the title of Arthur, for the Celtic high king performed the ritual functions of Arthur the sun god. The name of King Arviragus, who made the original grant of twelve hides to St Joseph, has been interpreted as meaning 'high king', and he may thus have been a personification of Arthur.

Apart from the leaden cross with its suspiciously convenient inscription, the account of the excavation seems to indicate a pre-Christian burial. The hollowed oak coffin is likely to have been one of the dugout canoes in which the old Glastonbury tribespeople navigated their inland waters, and the huge skull with its gaping hole had probably been trepanned.

The trepanning operation, as is known from Stone Age burials, was performed on certain people, often in their youth. This is inferred from the fact that in many cases the pierced bone has grown again over the

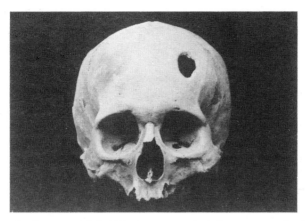

This example of a trepanned skull from an ancient burial site answers the description of King Arthur's holed skull, excavated by the monks at Glastonbury.

hole. Anthropologists say that trepanation is sometimes practised during initiation rituals, its purpose being to facilitate the flow of spirit through the mind of the initiate. These clues are merely tenuous, but they allow the possibility that the distinguished skeletons unearthed in 1190 belonged to no Christian king and queen—as it was necessary at that time to pretend—but were those of earlier, pagan rulers, whose history was one of the secrets of the Abbey.

The position of this ancient burial, and of the pillars that flanked it, would have been acknowledged within Glastonbury's esoteric foundation scheme. Neither of the pillars, however, stood where Bond located them. A later excavator, Dr Ralegh Radford, who continued Bond's archaeological work up to 1964, discovered their former sites on a line opposite the first bay to the east of the Lady Chapel's southern doorway. One of them was about forty feet and the other about sixty feet from the south wall of the chapel. Midway between them Radford uncovered the original tomb.

Bond was clearly wrong in claiming to have found one of the Arthurian pyramids. He later came to believe that the masonry he uncovered was the floor of an ancient bone house, built over the site of one of the twelve original founders' cells. Below the medieval stone-work he discerned traces of an earlier foundation, circular and about seven feet in diameter, and thus similar to the base of the pillar on the far side of the chapel. Unfortunately, Bond's disgrace and downfall, described in the next chapter, followed close upon his excavation of these two monuments. His diggings were hastily filled in and the enigmatic site to the south of the chapel has never since been investigated.

Whatever it was that Bond discovered, the occurrence of some ancient monument at that particular spot has proved to be of great interest, for it forms part of Glastonbury's original foundation pattern which the twelfth-century builders of St Mary's chapel artfully preserved.

Overleaf, above, is a diagram of the information given on the pillar, with the rectangular church of about 60 by 26 feet (outer measure) and the pillar 48 feet north of its centre line. This figure is like a mason's mark, which conveys something to the fraternity without revealing it to outsiders. From ancient to medieval times, Masonic craftsmen marked their works with symbols, usually consisting of a few lines at certain angles. These were the basic components of greater geometric schemes to which were attached certain meanings, and their full symbolism could be understood by those who knew the secrets of Masonic geometry.

No true source of Masonic lore is apparent today, and so, being uninitiated, we need further clues. They are amply provided by the plan of the stone chapel to St Mary which was said to have been completed no more than two years after the destruction of the Old Church. The speed with which this elaborate work was designed and executed suggests that the stone chapel had already been planned and was destined at some future time to complete the geometrical scheme inherent in the foundation pattern. When the plan of the St Mary chapel is laid over that of the wooden church, it can be seen how subtly the new building perpetuated the dimensions of the old, while adding further sets of proportions to the underlying design.

The significance of Bond's 'pyramid' site is now made plain. Together with the pillar and the western corners of the chapel, it provides one of the angles of a regular octagon, an eight-sided figure, geometrically defining the rectangle of St Mary's chapel.

From this pattern can be inferred the exact position and dimensions of St Joseph's wattle church. It lies at the centre of the diagram, at the east end of the chapel, and its diameter is equal to the chapel's inner width, 24 feet.

It will be seen that the dimensions given on the plan differ by small fractions from those recorded on the old pillar, which are expressed in whole numbers. There are good reasons for this, and they soon become apparent to those who study the esoteric tradition of number, music and geometry. The whole numbers are quite adequate in allowing an experienced geometer to reconstruct the scheme they refer to; an emphasis on precision would merely arouse idle curiosity. Moreover, in all such magical, cosmological structures there are deliberate ambiguities. The object of symbolic geometry was to make a synthesis of all musical harmonies and geometric proportions, expressed through the ratios of numbers, and thus to create a complete world-image. Taken literally, this task is obviously impossible, for the universe is a living reflection of its Creator, who is beyond rational enquiry, and its many levels can never be depicted together by any rational image. Yet, from the very beginning of civilization there has been known a certain numerical code or canon, which provides the best possible image of the universe, effective in attracting divine influences into the society that adopts it. The geometric structure which derives from that code was the basic foundation pattern at Glastonbury. It was supposed to contain all the different figures of geometry and to display in its dimensions all the numerical ratios that govern them. To achieve this within a rational, symmetrical work of architecture, such as the chapel at Glastonbury, the Masonic builders designed every feature to play its part in the overall scheme of proportions. Thus all the dimensions of the St Mary chapel had symbolic meaning, and all the basic figures of geometry were referred to in its inner and outer dimensions, which can be measured from various different points in the architecture, as is shown on the following pages.

One should not be surprised, therefore, to find that a site or building, designed in the sacred tradition, can be analyzed in terms of more than one scheme of geometry. The ambiguities are deliberate, for the

From the first wattle church to the 12th-century stone chapel of St. Mary, successive buildings at Glastonbury conformed to the same original groundplan. The evidence for this reconstruction of the foundation pattern comes from three main sources: the information on the dimensions of the Old Church given on the plaque attached to St. David's pillar, the actual dimensions of the St. Mary chapel and the tradition of cosmological proportions and measures associated with the Chinese Ming T'ang and other sacred structures. The likely development of the pattern is illustrated by the diagrams on the following pages.

The upper left diagram illustrates the information on the plaque affixed to St. David's pillar. The dimensions of the Old Church are there given in whole numbers. They are shown in the diagram, together with (in brackets below them) the exact measurements which they represent.

The inner dimensions of the wooden church are not stated. In accordance with masonic proportions, the outer dimensions are likely to have been greater by a tenth part of the inner dimensions. In that case the inner measurements of the church were 54 by 24 feet, making the inner area equal to 36^2 square feet (upper right diagram).

Also shown here are the positions of St. David's pillar, excavated by Bligh Bond in 1921, and of the 'pyramid' monument which Bond also discovered. They provide important clues to the fuller development of the foundation pattern.

Like the Ming T'ang, St. Joseph's wattle church was circular in imitation of the heavens, and it probably stood on a square platform or levelled patch representing the earth (below left). The traditional ratio between the widths of the circle and the square was 2:3. If the width of the square was 39.6 feet (a symbolic reference to the earth's radius of 3960 miles), the outer diameter of the circular church was therefore 26.4 feet. This is consistent with an inner diameter of 24 feet.

In the course of a few hundred years, the circular wattle wall of the church had no doubt decayed, and at some time during the Celtic period the sacred earth within it was protected by a rectangular wooden building (below right). Its eastern wall stood on the east end of the square platform. A second circle (shown in broken line) touching the original circle of the wattle church, determined the western limit of the rectangle. The length of the rectangle was therefore 59.4 feet, and its dimensions, 59.4 x 26.4 feet, made the area of the rectangle exactly equal to the area of the original, 39.6-foot-square platform.

The principal unit of measure in this scheme, producing integral numbers for all its dimensions, is equal to 1.32 feet, or a 500th part of a furlong.

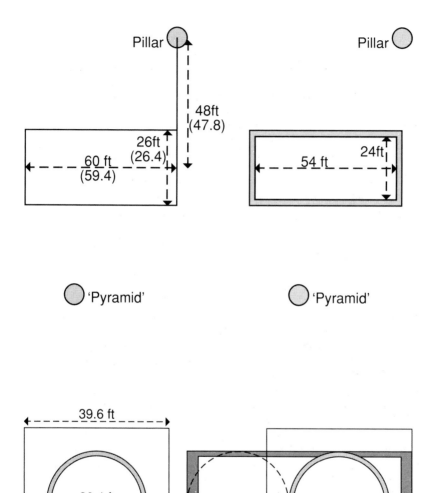

Pillar

48ft
(47.8)

26ft
(26.4)

60 ft
(59.4)

Pillar

54 ft

24ft

'Pyramid'

'Pyramid'

39.6 ft

26.4 ft

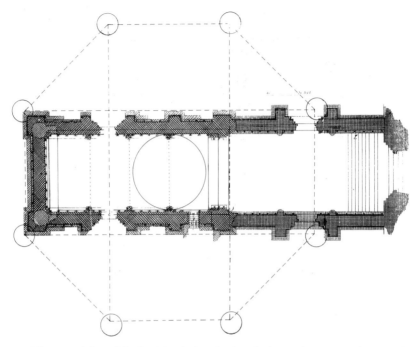

The groundplan of the St. Mary's chapel is here laid over the previous diagram of
the Old Church, showing how subtly the 12th-century builders recorded the proportions of the original scheme in the details of their architecture. The interior walls of
the chapel are divided into four bays by pillars at intervals of 13.2 feet (ten times the
unit of 1.32 feet). Midway between the first pair of pillars from the east end is the
central point of the circular wattle church and of the square on which it stood. The
central pair of pillars marks the western limit of the circle. The western side of the
original square platform coincides with the central line between the two doorways to
the chapel.

The positions of the pillar and 'pyramid', together with the western angles of the
chapel, produce a perfect octagon, centred upon the site of the wattle church. The side
of the octagon measures the same as the exterior width of the chapel, 39.6 feet. Its
interior width is equal to the inner diameter of the wattle church, 24 feet. The interior
length of the chapel, before its eastern wall was removed, was 52.8 feet, a hundredth
part of a mile. The recorded length of Glastonbury Abbey as a whole was 528 feet,
ten times the inner length of the chapel.

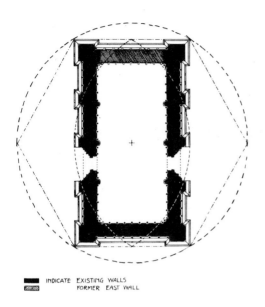

INDICATE EXISTING WALLS
FORMER EAST WALL

Bligh Bond's own geometric analysis of St. Mary's chapel (left) demonstrated its hexagonal proportions. This is not, however, the only possible interpretation. The two figures below show a hexagon and an octagon with sides of equal length, both containing the rectangular chapel. The width of the chapel being 39.6 feet, its theoretical length is 68.6 feet if its proportions are hexagonal, or 67.6 feet if they are octagonal. The slight projection of the chapel's corner towers accounts for the difference.

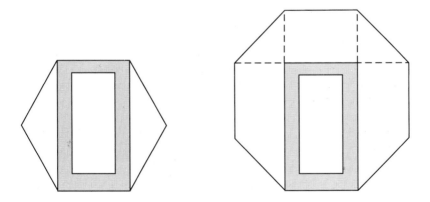

133

Masonic architects were skilled in contriving two or more sets of almost identical measurements, differing only by the width of a step or ridge, which suggested different geometric forms. An example is shown on page 133, where can be seen how narrow is the margin between the hexagonal and the octagonal significance of the proportions of the Saint Mary chapel. A similar coincidence between the twelve-sided and seven-sided shapes of geometry is illustrated in Chapter 15. The beauty of the Glastonbury scheme is that all its various shapes and measures are subsumed within a unifying pattern; and the pattern which emerges from these studies of Glastonbury's foundation is that traditional figure of cosmology, the image of heaven on earth, whose appearances are associated with a renewal of spirit and the achievement of the Grail.

Chapter Fourteen
The Glastonbury Revelations

The great pioneer in these studies of the esoteric significance of Glastonbury was Frederick Bligh Bond (1864-1945). During his period as director of excavations at the Abbey site, from 1909, he rediscovered many details of the ancient fabric, including the pillar and the monument referred to earlier, the Edgar chapel at the east end of the great church, the Loretto chapel and other architectural features previously unrecorded. The Church of England authorities, owners of the Abbey ruins, were gratified by his progress, but they were somewhat surprised by the excitement which the excavations seemed to be causing, and by the number of mystically inclined visitors who descended upon Glastonbury to inspect Bond's works.

Gradually strange rumours began to spread. Bligh Bond, they hinted, was in the grip of satanic forces. He had become obsessed with personal theories about the occult significance of the Abbey's dimensions, and his archeological works were conducted simply in order to prove them. These works were said to be guided by messages from spirits which Bond invoked during sessions of necromancy.

In appointing Bond to the Abbey ruins, his employers thought they had found just the right man for the job. He was an ecclesiastical architect, highly respected in his profession and known as an authority on medieval screens and church carvings, well versed in Glastonbury's lore and history, having read everything to be had on the subject. His manner was quiet and introspective and it was known that he held mystical views about the survival of the soul, but these peculiarities seemed tolerable at the time. Within a few years, however, Bond's activities had become quite intolerable as far as the Church was concerned. Dowsers, psychometrists and mediums were found to be directing the Abbey excavations, and Bond openly declared that his archaeological successes were achieved through information from the spirits of former monks.

In 1918 Bond published the full story of his Glastonbury experiments in *The Gate of Remembrance*. He revealed that, beginning in 1907, he and his friend, Captain John Allen Bartlett (referred to in the book as John Alleyne or J.A.), had been in regular contact with the spirit world through the medium of automatic writing. Captain Bartlett took down the messages as his hand was guided, while Bond put questions which were relevant to his Abbey researches. A remarkable effect of what they were doing was that it began to influence other psychics, some of whom knew nothing about Glastonbury. Once they had been invoked, Bond's informants, the Company of the Watchers of Avalon, spread their messages throughout the world of spirit mediums, and a constant series of revelations about the old Abbey, which often meant nothing to their recipients, were forwarded to Bligh Bond at Glastonbury. Many of these were nonsensical, but others were impressively coherent and gave likely details of Glastonbury lore and life in the days of the monks. The information they contained was often in direct response to questions which Bond was then pondering.

The malicious rumours of Bligh Bond's dealings with dark forces should have been laid to rest by the gentle, agreeably mystical tone of *The Gate of Remembrance*. Its leading character, speaking through the writing hand of Captain Bartlett, was a sixteenth-century Glastonbury monk, Johannes Bryant. He was a charming fellow, merry and simple-hearted and full of anecdotes about the old monkish life. In a mixture of archaic English and medieval Latin he told of fishing expeditions to the Meare lake, of the beauties of nature, the sweet birdsong on the Somerset Levels and the nutbrown ale at rustic revelries. One of his stories was of a visit to the Abbey by King Henry VIII. He and his court began an evening of roistering, and Johannes was sent to bring in another barrel of beer. While he was lowering it the rope broke and the barrel knocked Johannes to the ground. The king made a joke about drunken monks,

Frederick Bligh Bond

and thus poor Johannes felt himself partly responsible for Henry's suppression of the Abbey. It was, he insisted to Captain Bartlett, not his fault at all.

Johannes was no scholar and he had little to tell Bligh Bond about the foundation plan and esoteric traditions of Glastonbury Abbey. The deficiencies were made good by other Watchers, some of whom had lived in the early days of the Abbey and could speak with authority about its lost histories. They instructed Bond on where to dig, and the discoveries he made through following their advice gave credibility to their other pronouncements. Sometimes their memories failed, and some of their messages were garbled or contradictory, but the selection of inspired writings which Bond included in *The Gate of Remembrance* gives an attractive and plausible picture of old Glastonbury with significant hints at the nature of its underlying mystery.

Bligh Bond was an earnest philosopher in the mystical Platonic tradition. He was neither fanatical nor superstitious, and he was not inclined to believe in the survival of individual personalities after death. His monkish informants spoke as individuals, but Bond regarded them as voices from a group consciousness, a residue of the love and devotion which over the centuries had been concentrated on Glastonbury Abbey. He must have understood that the monks were to some extent projections of his own obsessions, especially when they claimed him as a reincarnation of one of the original twelve Glastonbury founders. It is known to all experienced writers, particularly those who enquire into mystical subjects, that mental concentration evokes corresponding data and phenomena from the world at large. This process can no doubt be expedited by spiritualistic methods such as Bond made use of; but these practices brought Nemesis upon him. A wretched scandal ensued from the publication of *The Gate of Remembrance*. Bond was driven under protest from his position at the Abbey, his excavations were filled in and all references to his discoveries were removed from the Abbey guide-book.

Cast out from his beloved Glastonbury, Bond was like a lost soul, and fate treated him accordingly. His enemies, led by his actively estranged wife, so blackened his reputation that his architectural practice dwindled away. He attempted various enterprises, such as editing a psychical

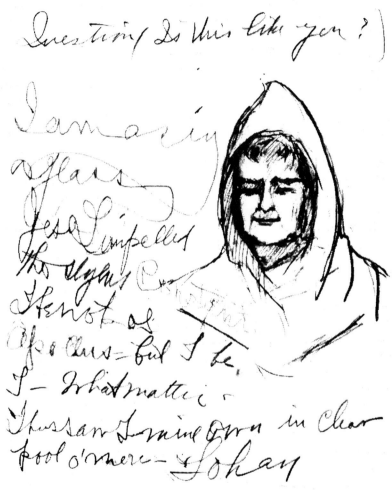

An inspired portrait of Johannes Bryant, the 16th-century Glastonbury monk whose spirit messages informed Bligh Bond's Gate of Remembrance. *The drawing was made by Mrs. Jessie Stevens in 1934. She asked Johannes, "Is this like you?" and received the reply by automatic writing, "I am as in a glass. Yes, I impelled the stylus. I be not as Apollus—but I be I—what matter? Thus saw I mine own in clear pool o' Mere. —Johan."*

research magazine, lecturing in America and even running a bed-and-breakfast house in Glastonbury for the reception of psychic visitors to the Abbey, but these also ended in failure. He constantly pondered the messages of the old monks and yearned to be allowed back on the Abbey site to re-establish contact with the Company. But the Glastonbury authorities were appalled by his notoriety and wanted nothing more to do with him. Exiled to a friend's refuge in North Wales, he died in bitterness and poverty.

The triumph and tragedies of Bligh Bond's career were equally linked to his spiritualistic activities. Through these he certainly achieved some remarkable insights into ancient Avalon—and not mere general impressions but detailed information, samples of which are reviewed below. Moreover, by his mental intensity Bond provoked a spiritual eruption at Glastonbury, whose effects have been significant and long-lasting. The most noticeable result of his psychic archaeology was that Glastonbury acquired a community of mystics. Some of the visitors to the Abbey excavations stayed on in the district. The Chalice Well was dedicated once more as a sanctuary. Artists and craftsmen found studios nearby, and the large house in Bovetown was opened as a school of music and drama by the famous composer, Rutland Boughton. English operas, Celtic plays and the cycle of Arthurian dramas were performed in the Assembly Rooms. Glastonbury for a time became known as the English Bayreuth and the focus of a mystical and mythological revival.

It has been suggested (by the Yeatsean scholar, Roger Parisious) that the mystical idealists who frequented Glastonbury during that period attempted to reconstruct and re-enact the Glastonbury ritual. Their inspiration came from W. B. Yeats and, through him, the Christian mystic, A. E. Waite.

It was in character for Yeats to have promoted a magical operation at Glastonbury, parallel to his work in Ireland. There he dreamed of founding a mystical Order, dedicated to performing the ritual for Ireland's regeneration. At Glastonbury the work would have been based on the Arthurian Grail cycle. Yeats was deeply versed in the Celtic mysteries. His knowledge of the old tradition, combined with the scholarly insights of Waite, informed Jessie Weston's book, *From Ritual to Romance*, which showed that the Grail legends evolved from a prehistoric rite, inherited by the Celtic Church.

Dion Fortune, whose book *Avalon of the Heart* describes some of the spiritual revivalist movements in Glastonbury at that time, is said by Parisious to have initiated a ritual there. Bond has also been claimed as a ritualist, and this is compatible with his growing obsession with finding the Holy Grail. During his Glastonbury period he was in touch with Yeats, who provided material for his *Apostolic Gnosis*. Yeats also introduced Bond to his favourite medium, Hester Dowden (Mrs. Travers Smith). She was much respected by discerning spiritualists for the clear, unselfconscious nature of her spirit communications, and was known also to the public through her remarkable book, *Psychic Messages from Oscar Wilde*. Bond enjoyed sessions with her towards the end of his Glastonbury career, and the results, as he said, were startling. Through her hand came a stream of narrative, far more coherent and suggestive than any of the scripts which Bond had previously received.

A product of Hester Dowden's automatic writing was a book which Bond published in 1932, *The Gospel of Philip the Deacon*. Bond asked for it to be judged on its literary merit, and by that standard alone it is a powerful work. Among its contents were the sublime narrative of Christ's Nativity, Passion and Resurrection, the story of Pentecost and the history of the Christian Grail vessel which St Joseph brought to England. According to this account, St Philip was one of his original twelve missionaries. St Joseph himself was the author, through Hester Dowden's mediumship, of another description of the foundation at Glastonbury, part of which was reproduced in Bond's *Company of Avalon*. It emphasized the relevance of symbolic numbers and measures to the Holy Rite performed in the wattle church.

Also from Bligh Bond's inspiration came the spate of booklets on Glastonbury's foundation and future destiny, such as Rev. L.S. Lewis's *St Joseph of Arimathea at Glastonbury* and the works of other mystical clergymen, mentioned in Chapter Nine. Lewis, who was Vicar of Glastonbury during the later years of Bond's excavations, warned him against spiritualism, though to no avail. Bond's downfall was undoubtedly caused by his obsession with spirit communications, but the churchmen who condemned him failed to submit his work to the test which is prescribed in the New Testament (I John, 4), "Believe not every spirit, but try the spirits whether they are of God." By that test, Bond's revelations came, if not from God, at least from no evil source. In the beauty of their language, as well as in their contents, the messages from the old monks reflected the quality of Bond's own mind. He himself was no poet, but the poems, stories and prophecies which he received through the hands of his mediums have authentic merit, whatever their origin. An example is the thrillingly mystical verse, transmitted through Captain Bartlett, which Bond appended to an illuminated address and presented to the Prince and Princess of Wales on their visit to Glastonbury in 1908:

> Then yͤ grasse shal bee as glasse
> And yͤ schal see yͤ mysterie
> Deep downe bit Iyes ffrom prynge eies
> And safelie slepes, while vigil kepes yͤ Company.
>
> (Howe doe) yͤ dry bonys stir and shake
> And eche to eche hys fellowe seekes
> Soone comes agayne what once hath bene
> And Glastonys glory shal be seene.

In the cases where Bond received practical information, as on the former dimensions of Glastonbury Abbey, the quality of his messages can be judged by a concrete standard, by whether or not they were accurate. There is little doubt that Bond's psychic archaeology was genuine, for there were many witnesses to his discoveries of unrecorded foundations exactly where his spirit guides had instructed him to dig.

Less easy to evaluate are the further series of dimensions which Bond was told about, those relating to the old wooden church and the Glastonbury foundation pattern.

In the latter part of Bond's life, the esoteric significance of those dimensions increasingly occupied his mind. He knew himself to be on the verge of a great discovery. All the clues were in his possession, but the secret of their proper arrangement, to give context and meaning to the foundation plan, was finally withheld from him.

Since Bond's time, the key to the secret has become apparent. The following chapter describes what Bond discovered—and what he missed—in his researches into the cosmological foundations of Glastonbury Abbey.

The Christian Revelation

Chapter Fifteen
The Stonehenge Prototype and the
Meaning of the Foundation Pattern

In describing the holiness which emanated from Glastonbury's Old Church and made its precinct "a heavenly sanctuary on earth", William of Malmesbury mentioned an enigmatic design on the stones of its floor.

> "One can observe there upon the paving, in the forms of triangles and squares, stones carefully interlaced and sealed with lead. If I believe that some sacred mystery is concealed under them, I do no harm to religion."

These words made a deep impression upon Bligh Bond. There is no other record of the pattern, and any part of it which survived the fire of 1184 was destroyed at the beginning of the sixteenth century when the floor of the chapel was removed to allow the construction of a crypt beneath it. Bond came to believe that the design on the floor was a mosaic representing the zodiac, a figure sometimes found in early churches. The twelve astrological signs would have been contained by the circle of the original wattle hut. It occurred to Bond that the twelve signs might also represented the twelve circular cells of St Joseph and his companions around the central church. The pattern on the floor would therefore have been a small-scale model of the Glastonbury foundation pattern.

In 1921, at the beginning of his last summer season of work on the

Abbey site, Bond was approached by a psychic lady, 'S'. She had been having visions of the ancient priory at Winchester, and the spirits of former monks had communicated with her through spontaneous writing. From them she learnt that in a former life she had been Brother Symon, the sub-prior at Winchester.

Bond was always suspicious of such claims, but he was intrigued by some of the spirit writings which S had been receiving, relating to Glastonbury. She had read *The Gate of Remembrance* because of her concern with spiritualism, but she was not concerned with the numbers and measures in the book and had paid them no attention. Yet in several of the messages which came to her were references to the Glastonbury foundation pattern and its mystical dimensions. These were the main subjects of Bligh Bond's next book, *The Company of Avalon*, published in 1924.

The chief informant of S's automatic scripts was Romualdus, who said he had been a monk at Glastonbury at the time of the great fire. He gave a vivid description of that event, and he complained that the new stone building which replaced the Vetusta Ecclesia (Old Church) did not have the same atmosphere of holiness. Measurements did not interest him at first, but he evidently realized that information on that subject was required, and by drawing on the memories of monks from older times he was able to give a picture of St Joseph's original settlement.

> "When Holie Ones first came: Chirche rounde in midst; Oure Lordes's Bodye on Awter, and round it, cubiculi XII, for Apostils, and lines—wayes—linea, going from cubiculi to Chirche. Doore of Chirche to Sud; in face thereof, cubiculi Sancti Joseph et Nataniel. Sanct Joseph was buried in Linea Bifurcata, menne say. Atte ende of eche waye a place in wall, so that eremites canne in Holie Place looke; no entering in save atte Masse. Alle this, in stane, on grounde of Ecclesia Vetusta menne sayde, so yatt menne sholde hit ne forgette."

Together with this message, the hand of S took down a rough sketch showing some of the twelve hermits' cells around the oratory.

This accorded with Bond's intuition that the first wattle church was circular and stood in the centre of a zodiac wheel, the twelve cells around it representing the twelve zodiacal signs. A similar account, published in *The Gate of Remembrance,* had previously reached him through Captain Bartlett:

> "That which the brethren of old handed down to us we followed, ever building on their plan. As we have said, our Abbey was a message in ye stones. In ye foundations and ye distances be a mystery—the mystery of our Faith, which ye have forgotten and we also in latter days. All ye measures were marked plaine on ye slabbes in Mary's Chapell and ye have destroyed them. So it was recorded, as they who builded and they who came after knew aforehand where they should build.

> "There was the body of Christ, and round Him would have been the Four Ways. Two were ybuilded and no more. In ye floor of ye Mary Chappel was ye Zodiac, that all might see and understand the Mystery. In the midst of ye Chappel He was laid . . ."

Similar information came to Bond spontaneously from other sources. Most impressive were the automatic scripts obtained from an American medium who knew nothing at all about Glastonbury or the early church in England. Yet, when asked about St Joseph's foundation, he immediately responded with relevant statements, including the following:

> "Joseph did build, as ye have said, in a circle: but Patric and David did renovate his building.

> "As the years passed by, many listened to the words of Joseph. And they that were most venerable among the Druids received the Word with reverence; for hidden beneath their ancient rites lay truths so deep and simple

that the people could not comprehend their beauty.

"As to the floor, of course ye know the central figure—
the Cross—the Circle—the Universe. Then the Four
Ways to Christ which were through the Great Four.
Also the Signs of the Zodiac—for the Names of sacred
Things are known to the stars; in the number of their
letters, in the spelling out of future events. You know
that in the designing of the Floor lies the future
prophecy of Glastonbury, together with the inward
secrets of Christianity."

This message obviously reflected Bligh Bond's obsessions, and the
spirit writer made this plain by referring to Bond by name as the author
of an interesting book, *The Apostolic Gnosis*. He had indeed written such
a book, in collaboration with one of the mystical clergymen who
frequented Glastonbury, Rev. T. Simcox Lea. *The Apostolic Gnosis* was
an inquiry into the esoteric code of number and geometry which
underlies the forms of sacred architecture and can also be discovered,
through the techniques of gematria (the translation of letters into
numbers), in the books of the Old and New Testaments. As soon as
Bond became immersed in this subject, references to number and
gematria began to appear in his friends' spirit writings.

One can not help seeing that much of the information which Bond
was given by the spirits coincided with intuitions which had already
formed in his mind. This was particularly evident in the later part of his
career. Yet even though his own will and imagination may to some
extent have conditioned the spirit messages, that does not necessarily
invalidate their contents. Bond knew more about Glastonbury, and had
a deeper insight into its past, than anyone else of his time. He was
uniquely qualified to understand the occult significance of the numbers
and measurements which the spirits imparted to him. He had prepared
himself for revelation, he invoked it, and when it came he was its natural
recipient.

In these chapters we are not so much concerned with Bond's
methods as with his results. Wherever it came from, the information he

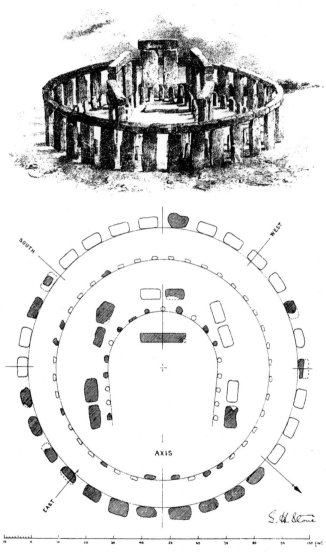

Stonehenge reconstructed and its groundplan.
The stones still standing are shaded in the plan (after Stone).

149

obtained was fairly presented; it can be assessed on its own terms, and the further one studies the material of Bond's revelations, the more one learns to respect it. Step by step, Bond was guided towards the crowning revelation of his career at Glastonbury. The clues began pointing in a certain direction, towards Stonehenge, and Bond began to follow them there. Had he continued on that course, he would surely have come to realize that in the plan of Stonehenge is the key to the mystery of Glastonbury.

The Christian settlement at Glastonbury, so Bond was told, occupied the site of a former pagan sanctuary, and its dimensions reproduced those of a certain ancient temple in the West of England. Cornwall was the indicated region, and when Bond found the place-name, Temple, on Bodmin Moor, he suggested that the earlier temple might have been located there. Stonehenge certainly came to his mind in connection with Glastonbury. In one of his *Glastonbury Scripts*—episodes in the history of the Abbey as related by its former monks—is a versified account of how St Joseph walked from Glastonbury to Stonehenge to converse with the Druids at their great temple. They were impressed when he showed them the groundplan of his Christian settlement, recognizing it as similar to their own foundation pattern. Yet, despite all his clues and intuitions, Bond somehow never thought to make a direct comparison between the revealed dimensions of the Glastonbury site and the design of Stonehenge.

A geometrical link between these two sites was first suggested by the writer and architect, Keith Critchlow. At the behest of Janette Jackson, a life-long advocate of Bligh Bond and his Glastonbury theories, Critchlow reviewed Bond's findings, as set out in *The Company of Avalon*, and published his report in *Britain: a Study in Patterns*, a book of essays which Mrs Jackson edited in 1970. He showed that the system of proportions which Bond had observed in the St Mary chapel at Glastonbury applied also to the groundplan of Stonehenge. In the settings of the ancient stones he found evidence of an underlying scheme which synthesized the basic figures of geometry—squares, circles, octagons, pentagons and others. Critchlow had read Soothill's *Hall of Light* and agreed with him in seeing an analogy between the Stonehenge temple and the Chinese Ming T'ang. A similar design of proportions and symbolic measures was expressed in both their foundation plans.

It can now be shown (with the closest approach to certainty that is possible in these matters) that Stonehenge and Glastonbury were both founded on the same pattern. This does not imply that the Glastonbury founders copied the plan of the ancient temple, but rather, that the same traditional model was used in both cases. It is impossible to say whether that model was transmitted by a freemasonry of temple builders over the two thousand years which separate Stonehenge from Glastonbury, or whether it was renewed by revelation at the beginning of the Christian era. However one explains it, the evident fact is that both Stonehenge and Glastonbury share a common groundplan.

Both the Glastonbury foundation pattern and the restored groundplan of Stonehenge have been illustrated previously. Overleaf, the two are placed together on the same scale, and their identical nature is made plain in the caption.

The most remarkable aspect to the story of Bligh Bond and his spirit messages is that he never consciously recognized the connection between Glastonbury and Stonehenge. Yet it was presented to him very plainly in a script which came on an auspicious day, the feast of St Michael the revealer of mysteries, in 1921.

Ambrosius speaks:

> "First let there be a Circle—ronde CXXX paces— gressus: on it XII cubiculi. Ronde outer, CCCLX. with fence. In midst of all, Ronde Chirche, but XVIII. crosst: wall of mudd and stane III. thick—total XXIV. in your measures.

> "Outer fence in olde measures, by steppes—paces. Celles not all equal in ring: two at sud—linea bifurcata—lo! I have thee shown aforetyme; because of grunde. But near equal."

In this are described three concentric circles. The ring at the centre represents St Joseph's oratory. Its dimensions are given in our measures, presumably feet, confirming that its outer diameter was 24 feet.

The middle circle marked the ring of twelve hermits' cells. Its circumference is given as about 130 paces. A pace is equal to 2½ feet, so the circle measured about 325 feet round.

The circumference of the third, outer circle is 360 paces "in olde measures." This implies that the foot unit, of which there were 2½ to the pace, was not the modern English foot.

One of our ancient British measures was the so-called Roman foot, which was not in fact of Roman origin but was known long before classical times. It was shorter only by a small fraction than the English foot, its defined length being .9732 English feet. A unit of that length was used in the building of Stonehenge, where the inner circumference of

The plan of the Glastonbury chapel with its octagonal geometry is placed together with the groundplan of Stonehenge, both drawn on the same scale, and the common origin of the two schemes is immediately apparent. The angles of the octagon lie upon the lintels of the sarsen ring, and the line which limits the upper end of the chapel marks the end of the U or vessel shape formed by the five pairs of trilithons. The parallel line between the two angles of the octagon is tangent to the inner vessel formation of standing stones, and the semi-circle at the base of the vessel has a width equal to that of the St Mary chapel, 39.6 feet. A circle of twice that width, 79.2 feet, touches the inside wall at the lower end of the chapel and coincides with the Stonehenge circle of bluestones.

Eight times 39.6 feet is 316.8 feet, or a hundredth part of 6 miles, and that is the measure round the eight sides of the Glastonbury octagon. 316.8 feet also measures the mean circumference of the Stonehenge sarsen ring. The important symbolism of the number 3168 is examined in previous books (for example, The Dimensions of Paradise*).*

The same foundation plan was developed in quite different ways at Stonehenge and Glastonbury though always in accordance with the proportions inherent in the original design. At both sites, the first structure was a circular wooden hut for a shamanic or priestly astronomer. It measured 24 feet in diameter, and the platform on which it stood was 39.6 feet square. At Stonehenge a large circular building of wood and thatch was erected to cover the original site, and this was replaced in about 2000 B.C. by the existing stone rings. The sacred centre was protected by two stone formations shaped like vessels, which opened towards the north-east to receive the light of the rising midsummer sun. At Christian Glastonbury the development was rectangular, but the builders of St Mary's chapel adhered to the same traditional scheme of proportions as the Stonehenge builders.

the sarsen circle measures 100 'Roman' feet exactly.

The dimensions of the two circles seem therefore to be:

Circle with huts, about 130 paces = 325 feet
Outer circle, 360 Roman paces = 876 feet

These two circles are of the same dimension as two of the principal circles at Stonehenge (the sarsen circle and the ring of Aubrey holes). Not recognizing that fact, Bond was puzzled by the figures given in the script. At the time when he received this message, he was immersed in a study of symbolic number, and this influenced his interpretation. By

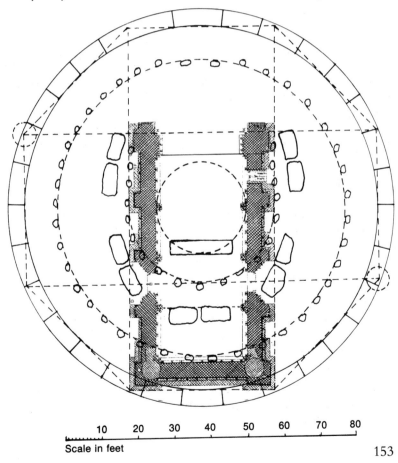

10   20   30   40   50   60   70   80

Scale in feet

153

using two different approximations to the Roman pace, he obtained the numbers which he felt most appropriate. Thus his estimate for the circumference of the outer circle was 888 ft. (the number 888 signifying by gematria the name of Jesus), and of the inner 314.1 ft. or a hundred times π ('pi').

Bond pointed out that the two circles of 130 and 360 paces are linked together geometrically by a twelve-pointed star. In the diagram below, it is seen that an identical result is obtained through the geometry of the seven-pointed star or heptagram. As Critchlow demonstrated, many different schemes of proportion can be discovered in Stonehenge, and that is in accordance with the traditions of sacred architecture. The various rings at Stonehenge were spaced at intervals which marked the nodes or meeting points of different geometric figures, small discrepancies being accommodated within the widths of the rings. The result was no rough compromise but an artful synthesis of all the numbers, harmonies, proportions and measures by which God was conceived to have constructed the universe. As a rationalized world-image, Stonehenge provides evidence for the numerous astronomical, geometric and other theories which have been projected upon it. None of these are necessarily wrong; they only become so when they are offered as definitive, exclusive interpretations.

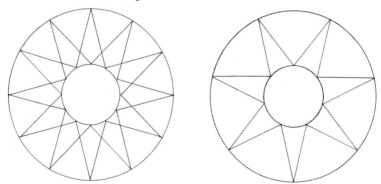

Two concentric circles, representing the sarsen stone circle and the ring of Aubrey holes at Stonehenge, can be linked geometrically by either a twelve-pointed or a seven-pointed star. Calculations show that there is virtually no theoretical difference between the proportions of the two sets of rings.

One of Bligh Bond's spirit messages included a sketch plan of the Glastonbury chapel containing the circle of St. Joseph's church. It gave a hint—ignored by Bond—that the site of the original church was at the east end rather than in the centre of the chapel.

It is evident that in one respect Bond's reconstruction of St Joseph's settlement at Glastonbury was misconceived. His spirit guides never informed him on the exact position of the original circular church, and he assumed without question that it was centrally placed within the walls of St Mary's chapel. If that had been the case, part of its patterned floor would have overlapped the passageway between the north and south doors of the chapel, and pilgrims filing through those doors would have trodden on the sacred earth they had come to venerate. It is more natural to assume that visitors looked eastwards down the length of the chapel and that the relic lay near its east end. The position of the wattle church is clearly indicated by the geometry of the site, and it is just where one would expect to find it, below the altar at the east end of the chapel. This is confirmed by the comparison of the Glastonbury and Stonehenge groundplans on page 153, where the circle representing the round church is seen to lie within the inner sanctum at the centre of all.

By the end of his Glastonbury career, Bond's researches had become centred on the problem of locating the sites of the twelve hermits' cells occupied by St Joseph and his companions. These cells, so the scripts told him, were placed around the wattle church in a circle whose circumference was said to be 130 paces or some 325 feet. When they decayed, their sites were marked by small chapels or monuments. Two of the sites were identified in the scripts; one was occupied by the chapel of St Dunstan to the west of St Mary's chapel, and the other was opposite it to the east, at the altar of the Galilee chapel. From further hints Bond concluded that the sites of two other cells were denoted by the stone pillar to the north of the Old Church and by the 'pyramid' which he excavated on the south side.

In his attempt to draw a circle of the given measure, linking the sites of the ancient cells, Bond was frustrated by his misconception about the position of the original wattle church at the centre of the pattern. He located it in the middle rather than at the east end of St Mary's chapel, but a circle from that centre can not pass through both the pillar and the pyramid sites. No symmetrical pattern of cells was apparent, and Bond was forced to conclude that the cells were irregularly spaced in a very approximate ring around the church. This vague formation was incompatible with the precise measures he was given in the script, nor did it accord with his idea of a symmetrical zodiac wheel.

The most obvious figure in the esoteric geometry of Glastonbury is the octagon. Of its eight angles two fall on the sites of the pillar and the pyramid, while two others mark corners of the rectangular chapel. If Bond's intuition was correct, each of the eight angles would give the position of one of the cells. The cells, however, were not eight but twelve in number. An astrological arrangement would place them in four groups of three, corresponding to the three months in each of the four seasons. The diagram opposite shows how the twelve cells could have been placed symmetrically within the framework of the octagon. This arrangement, where the four cells at the cardinal points stand outside the main ring on the corners of the square containing the octagon, seems best in accordance with the aesthetics of geometry. It also allows one of the cells to occupy the east end of St Dunstan's chapel, as indicated by Bond's script. Another lies beneath the steps at the east of the Galilee, and a third, south of the chapel, occupies the most important site of all. It lies opposite the first bay in the chapel wall to the east of the doorway, and some 50 feet distant from it. On that very site Dr Radford rediscovered the legendary tomb of King Arthur which the monks had opened after the great fire.

According to Bond's information, the southernmost cell on the Glastonbury settlement was that of St Joseph himself. Thus the same key spot in the foundation pattern around St Mary's chapel is associated with

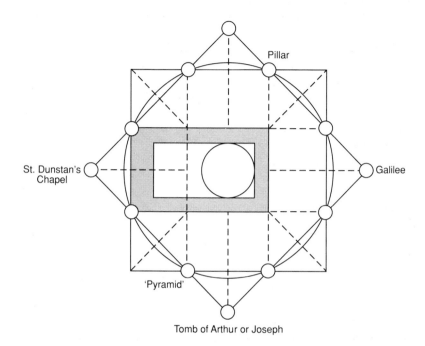

St. Dunstan's Chapel

Pillar

Galilee

'Pyramid'

Tomb of Arthur or Joseph

The foundation pattern at Glastonbury is suggested in the above diagram. Eight of the cells occupied by St. Joseph's followers were sited on the eight corners of an octagon. The sides of the octagon were extended, thus producing two overlapping squares. On the four corners of one of the squares were placed the remaining four cells. The burial place of St. Joseph beneath the southernmost cell on a 'linea bifurcata', is on the site where the Glastonbury monks claimed to have found the tomb of King Arthur.

The circle passing through eight of the cells has its circumference equal to the measure round the eight sides of the octagon. That distance is 316.8 feet (a hundredth part of six miles) which is also the measure of the mean circumference of the Stonehenge sarsen circle. The walls of St. Mary's chapel, containing the circle of St. Joseph's wattle church, are here shaded.

157

two leading figures in the Glastonbury saga, King Arthur and St Joseph of Arimathea.

Had he been allowed to continue his excavations, Bond was confident that he would have discovered the ring of cells, the tomb of St Joseph and buried treasures of Glastonbury Abbey, including the vessel of the Holy Grail. His need for such material discoveries arose from his commitment to spiritualism. The only sure way of vindicating his archaeological methods, and psychic research generally, was to reveal some awesomely precious object through the guidance of spirit messages. Thus was Bond led downwards into literalism and diverted away from Glastonbury's real treasure, the philosopher's stone which is traditionally located in the Abbey precinct. In the sixteenth century, soon after the Abbey's dissolution, the sage John Dee sought the stone among its ruins, and is said to have learnt its secrets with the aid of his spirit medium, Edward Kelley. Bond was also guided towards the philosopher's stone. That is evident from the nature of his studies during his period at Glastonbury. He was attracted by a subject almost entirely unknown in his time, the science of number symbolism, which provides the foundation of all esoteric sciences. Through this study, rather than through psychic archaeology and the search for actual cells, Bond made his nearest approach towards the heart of the Glastonbury mystery.

Medieval pilgrims to Glastonbury were rewarded by the sight of ancient relics, the holy thorn tree, the wooden church and other mementos of St Joseph's mission. The foundation legend, as promulgated at the Abbey, was adapted to their simple faith, and they were told about twelve holy men who journeyed to pagan Britain and, through the example of their pious lives, won the country folk over to Christ. It is an archetypal story with parallels, as we have seen, in many different traditions, both pagan and Christian. But it was not, as we have also seen, an adequate description of how Christianity was actually established at Glastonbury. The truth of what happened was too mystical and too deeply rooted in pre-Christian magic to provide the popular account of Glastonbury's legend. The average pilgrim would have known or cared nothing about number, geometry, sacred measures and the priestly arts. Yet the holy atmosphere which the pilgrims to the Abbey came to experience was sustained by these arts; and they in turn were derived from a traditional code of wisdom, transmitted through the Mystery schools and symbolized by the philosopher's stone.

The quest at Glastonbury is not merely for cells, tombs, an ancient church or a precious vessel. These objects are guiding symbols and point to something that lies beyond them, to Glastonbury's real treasure. Bligh Bond's later guidance was towards a greater prize than can be acquired through archaeology. He was led to see a foundation pattern, a harmonious structure of magical, cosmological numbers, as the essential feature of Glastonbury's Christian settlement. This pattern is now more clearly discernible, and it proves also to be the foundation pattern of Stonehenge.

The Glastonbury legend is an allegory, attuned to different levels of understanding. At every level it is true, and at its core can be imagined the greatest of all truths, capable of transforming individuals and whole societies. Progress towards the centre is through the veils which separate the various stages of initiation. The first stage is easy enough. Without doubting the simple truth of the St Joseph legend, we can see behind it the archetypal story of twelve founding saints or twelve heroes as in the court of Arthur. The foundation legend is thus loosened from its historical Christian setting, and is perceived to be a universal legend, describing the origins of many different religions.

Having seen beyond the surface of St Joseph's legend, we are no longer searching for relics but for meaning. At the foundation of Glastonbury was a long-sustained priestly ritual which breathed new life into the countryside. It amounted to an invocation of the Holy Grail, and its mythic framework is reflected in the cycle of Grail romance. Another survival of the ancient ritual is the foundation pattern, which contributed to the ritual and expressed its primary purpose, to produce a heavenly sanctuary on earth. Confronted with the foundation pattern, we enter upon a new stage in the quest, for that pattern has a cosmological significance, and those who study it are drawn towards a closer understanding of the traditional world-view which included in harmony all the elements in God's creation. Without that understanding we can approach no nearer towards the centre of the Glastonbury mystery.

The pattern which has been discerned at Glastonbury, and the same pattern at Stonehenge and other religious foundations, is not the end of the quest. It represents indeed the beginning of the most laborious stage in the process of initiation, the time of study, when those who wish to proceed further are introduced to the numerical basis of the divine knowledge to which they aspire.

That knowledge today is completely hidden, and even its very existence is not generally recognized. It is not therefore easy to study it. Nor is it necessary to do so in order to enjoy a useful, happy life. As Plato allowed, simple faith in the goodness of creation is an adequate substitute for the divine knowledge. Yet those who acquire that knowledge, continues Plato, sanctify both themselves and their whole environment. That knowledge, whenever and wherever it reappears, creates a renewal of spirit and culture which amounts to a new revelation or vision of the Holy Grail. Those who embark on the Grail quest only do so because they have glimpsed a distant light which then seems to be the only thing in the world worth achieving. The guiding light is provided for us by the Glastonbury prophecies, which hint at the unlimited benefits which will follow when Glastonbury finally reveals her treasure.

Chapter Sixteen
Glastonbury in the Light of Prophecies

The most mystical of Glastonbury's ancient records is the Prophecy of Melkin. It was quoted in John of Glastonbury's *Chronicle* from a book of ancient British histories, now lost, which is known to have existed in the Abbey library before the Dissolution. Probably the last person to read Melkin's book was the historian, John Leland, an agent of Henry VIII, who spent twelve years going round all the great monastic and other libraries throughout England and Wales in order to examine their contents. When he reached Glastonbury, Abbot Whiting opened the library to him, and Leland was immediately excited by what he saw there. "Scarcely had I crossed the threshold," he wrote,"when the mere sight of the most ancient books seized my mind with awe and a kind of stupor, and for that reason I was stopped in my tracks for a while. Then, having paid my respects to the deity of the place, I examined all the bookcases for some days with the greatest interest." One of the writings which specially drew his attention was a fragment of Melkin's *History of the Britons*.

The mysterious Melkin is commonly identified as the Welsh bard and chieftain, Maelgwn of Gwynedd, who died in 547. He was thus a contemporary of that heroic King Arthur whose deeds, assimilated with those of the ever-living mythical Arthur, were celebrated in the old chronicles. Early references to Melkin associate him with Merlin and with the British prophecy that the kingdom of Arthur will one day be restored. He was also credited with a history of King Arthur and the Round Table.

By the fourteenth century, when John of Glastonbury repeated it, Melkin's Prophecy had been translated, adapted and added to by a succession of copyists, and had lost much of its original sense. As it now stands it is incomplete and garbled, but it contains some ancient and important clues to the essential mystery of Glastonbury.

The Prophecy comes to us in Latin from the original Welsh. In James Carley's literal translation it reads:

> "The Isle of Avalon, greedy in the burial of pagans, above others in the world, decorated at the burial place of all of them with vaticinatory little spheres of prophecy, and in future it will be adorned with those who praise the Most High. Abbadare, powerful in Saphat, most noble of pagans, took his sleep there with 104,000. Among them, Joseph de Marmore, named 'of Arimathea' took everlasting sleep. And he lies on a forked line (*linea bifurcata*) close to the southern corner of the chapel with prepared wattle above the powerful venerable Maiden, the thirteen aforesaid sphered things occupying the place. For Joseph has with him in the tomb two white and silver vessels filled with the blood and sweat of the prophet Jesus. When his tomb is found, it will be seen whole and undefiled in the future, and will be open to all the earth. From then on, neither water nor heavenly dew will be able to be lacking for those who inhabit the most holy island. For a long time before the Day of Judgement in Josaphat will these things be open and declared to the living."

As Carley points out, there are obvious eastern and Islamic references in this text, probably introduced at the time of the Crusades. John of Glastonbury indeed quotes the prophecy in connection with the story of Reinald of Marksbury (north of Glastonbury near Bath) who travelled to the Holy Land, was captured by a Sultan and gained his friendship by paying a ransom of holy earth from the Glastonbury cemetery. The Sultan evidently knew of St Joseph, for he inquired about his burial place, between the two pyramids south of the St Mary's chapel, and acknowledged him as the man who had taken the body of the prophet Jesus from the Cross. This same, typically Islamic reference to the "prophet Jesus" occurs also in the Prophecy of Melkin, together with other such eastern names as Abbadare (Abu Adar?), Josaphat and Saphat. The last name can be read as Safad, a centre of cabalistic learning and a stronghold of the Knights Templar in the Holy Land.

The Prophecy of Melkin, as Carley also remarks, has a strong alchemical flavour. The reference to heavenly dew is to that *ros coeli* of the Rosicrucians which distills the pure gold and is symbolized by the droplets in St Joseph's coat of arms. In keeping with the eastern character of the Prophecy is the promise of "water and heavenly dew" to the inhabitants of the Isle of Avalon. Superficially, this offers little benefit to those who live in watery Somerset, but the phrase did not originate there. It makes more sense in arid Jerusalem, and one of the legends of the Jerusalem Temple is that, when the Jews rebuild it, water and heavenly dew are among the blessings which shall follow. Symbolized by the phrase are the happiness and prosperity which traditionally follow upon the restoration of the Grail.

In the prophecies of Glastonbury those blessings are linked to the discovery of St Joseph's body and of something which was buried with him. Melkin's text has suffered medieval interpolation, and the "vessels filled with the blood and sweat of the prophet Jesus" have replaced the original object which was no doubt of pagan symbolism. Clearly it was a symbol of the Holy Grail. It was therefore a bowl or chalice, a receptacle for divine grace. Some such vessel once stood at the centre of St Joseph's wattle church and provided the focus for the rituals performed by the twelve holy men. The form of their operation was similar to that of the alchemists in performing the Great Work. The object in both cases was the same, to redeem the earth and restore it to its natural condition as a paradise, and at the centre of all such operations was a receptacle which symbolized the work and reflected its progress— a chalice, a crystal jewel or an alchemical retort. Glastonbury Abbey in the Middle Ages claimed to possess more than one vessel with the mystical attributes of St Joseph's talisman, but the original vessel was buried in Joseph's tomb, and the site of that tomb was either unknown to the Glastonbury monks or never openly revealed. An old Glastonbury legend said that Joseph was buried at Montacute, a few miles south of the Abbey, where a hill dedicated to St Michael has features in common with Glastonbury's St Michael's Tor. According to Melkin, however, he lies in a *linea bifurcata* at Glastonbury's Old Church.

These Latin words have always been a puzzle to scholars. One version of their translation has it that Joseph was buried in a divided linen shirt, but the meaning commonly accepted is that his tomb was on a mysterious 'forked line' in the Abbey cemetery. A line is a geometric term, and the reference here is presumably to a junction of two lines in the geometry of Glastonbury's foundation pattern.

In one of the genuinely ancient parts of Melkin's Prophecy is a further allusion to the foundation pattern. The thirteen prophetic little spheres which are said to occupy the holy site at Glastonbury have been interpreted, by Carley and others, as the twelve signs of the zodiac around a thirteenth sphere at the centre. Melkin's system of spheres could therefore describe the pattern of the inlaid stones on the floor of Glastonbury's Old Church, mentioned by William of Malmesbury and imagined by Bligh Bond to have formed the wheel of a zodiac.

The legend that some powerful and precious relic lies buried at Glastonbury—at the site of the Abbey, on Chalice Hill or somewhere else nearby—appears to have been long established in local folklore. It forms one item in that web of tradition which links Glastonbury with the age-old prophecy of the golden age restored, of the recovery of the Grail, the reappearance of Arthur's Round Table or the coming of Christ's kingdom on earth. Such dreams of the millennial archetype seem naturally to concentrate upon Glastonbury. Their fulfilment will presumably be in accordance with different levels of expectation, including the physical plane. Many precious objects are thought to be concealed around the district, in old farms and manor houses of the Abbey estate or in tunnels and secret chambers beneath the town. Monks are notorious for hiding things away; Glastonbury possessed relics and manuscripts not disclosed to the laity, which had vanished by the time of the Dissolution, and the official charge against the last abbot, Whiting, was of concealing Abbey treasures. To do so was, indeed, his most sacred duty. It is not unlikely, therefore, that when times are ripe, something wonderful will be unearthed at Glastonbury, a portent of more significant revelations to follow.

A treasure trove of ancient artifacts or writings would cause a nine-day wonder before disappearing into some museum or archive. Yet such a discovery would have deeper repercussions, turning minds towards the Glastonbury prophecies and the meaning of their fulfilment. Even to contemplate that meaning is to be exposed to mental transformation, for on every level the message of Glastonbury is unequivocally the same. Behind all the legends, prophecies and revelations at Glastonbury can be discerned one single theme: that the will of God will finally prevail, and humanity will rediscover its natural condition within an earthly paradise.

This interpretation can be proved by reference to Glastonbury's foundation pattern. It has been shown to be the same pattern as lies at the foundation of Stonehenge, and this implies that the Christian settlement at Glastonbury at the beginning of the age of Pisces had the same general purpose as the Stonehenge temple at the beginning of Aries. Stonehenge has many mysteries, but its purpose is not mysterious, for it is clearly spelt out in the form and symbolism of its groundplan. The source of the Stonehenge plan and its dimensions is a traditional geometric figure, laid out to a certain scale in accordance with a certain numerical formula and based on the symbol of marriage between heaven and earth, the 'squared circle.' It is described in outline in the previous chapter, and it can be studied in further detail in the author's earlier books, listed in the Bibliography. This combination of circle, square and other geometric shapes represents the heavenly order, reduced to the level of reason and thus made applicable to the order of human life on earth. From the earliest times of civilization it has provided the model for temples and ideal cities, real and imaginary. Its dimensions are those in which Plato drew up his image of the most just and balanced form of society, and they were later referred to by St John, in Revelation 21, as the measurements of the celestial city which he saw in a vision as it descended into material reality. Behind this image is the twelve-fold numerical scheme, the archetype of all the twelve-tribe kingdoms and groups of twelve sacred heroes mentioned in earlier chapters. Its pattern was copied at the foundation of Arthur's Round Table, in the social order of early Celtic Britain and in the design of the first Christian settlement at Glastonbury. It is a symbol of a recurrent revelation, when the ideals which inspire the Grail quest are once again made visible.

This figure of an ideal universe is a truer symbol of the Grail than any mere physical object, but it is still just a symbol. Its function is to bring a sense of proportion to the minds of those who contemplate it, preparing them for the next stage in the quest. We have thus been guided into a process of initiation. It is the classical process, as undergone in the ancient Mysteries, and one of its stages involves the study of number in its true, cosmological aspect. That study was essential in the Pythagorean, Druidic and ancient Mystery schools generally, but there are said to be many paths towards initiation, and enlightenment is not always the product of studies in symbolic number. Those who feel adapted to the subject are assured by tradition of mental and spiritual benefits therefrom. The path they follow is well trodden and it can lead to wisdom. It is not, however, the only way, and those who are not attracted to it may travel further and more pleasantly by other routes.

The puzzling, unfamiliar yet wonderfully exciting conclusion which is forced upon us by examination of the Glastonbury mystery is that we are being asked to contemplate an alternative reality, a reality quite unacknowledged by modern habits of thought, the reality of a heavenly order on earth. That is the ideal which appeals to and links all humanity. It may now sound unreal, but it was not considered so in many different ages in the past, and it seems beyond doubt to be the only practical ideal and image for the present circumstances. The paradisial world-view is optional, but it is natural, primeval and constantly recurring to the mind and imagination. Its credentials testify to its reality, and its desirability— its necessity even—are beyond question. The secret of Glastonbury is that we are invited to enter an earthly paradise.

As an abstract ideal, paradise on earth has a universal attraction, but the question of its actual form gives rise to a multiplicity of images. It is something that everyone wants, but no one knows exactly what it is. The only profitable way of examining it, therefore, is on the level of its own, abstract reality. On that level it can be imagined as a universal harmony, an intensified combination of all the sounds, scents, forms and colours which most delight the senses. Inherent in it is the idea of perfect relationships between every particle in God's creation—a state which already exists, whether or not we choose to perceive it. Once that fact becomes evident, its power for transformation is irresistible.

One of the conventional symbols of earthly paradise is the union between two cities, the heavenly Jerusalem and the actual city of Jerusalem below. William Blake drew on that image in prophesying that the New Jerusalem would first become manifest in England. He formed that conviction partly from his studies of Stonehenge, Avebury and the Glastonbury legends, and he was certainly in earnest when he proclaimed it. He did not, however, produce any groundplan or constitution for an ideal society. Blake was a poet, not a politician, and his imagination was effective on the highest level, in illuminating the idea of paradise and establishing it in the minds of his contemporaries.

Plato was more practical minded than Blake, and he had the privilege of access to the ancient scholarly traditions on the achievement of an earthly paradise. He was thus qualified to express the ideal in more concrete terms. His imaginary republic was based on the archetype of heavenly paradise, and from there he descended into the world of matter, interpreting the ideal in the form of a social order which he considered to be its best possible reflection. Due to its material nature, Plato's republic was necessarily structured and was governed by a code of laws. It was, as Plato admitted, a mere third-hand version of the ideal, for the original is the heavenly archetype, and its clearest reflection on earth is that primordial paradise, remembered in the story of the Garden of Eden and experienced by the wandering tribespeople of ancient Avalon. From that paradise we have long been barred due to the necessary inhibitions of civilization. Most people today enjoy the civilized state and its comforts, and therefore, like Plato, we are concerned in practice with the second-hand reflection of paradise, a perfectly ordered, permanently settled human society. It is not the innocent paradise of Eden, but it is the next best thing, and Plato promised that, if its standards were scrupulously maintained, it would be almost as good and as long-lasting as the original.

The numerical cosmology from which Plato derived the forms of his republic is also discovered at the foundation of the Glastonbury settlement. It offers no building plan for an ideal city or constitution, but it does indicate the way of thought through which these and other benefits may be acquired. Such benefits are not to be gained by human ingenuity alone, nor by any man-made utopian contrivances. The ideal pattern is ready-made and comes from above. It enters the mind as an archetype which takes shape as a symbol, and thence it descends down the scale of human consciousness into the sphere of concrete reality. It is not invented but invoked.

Thus the work performed by the first Christians at Glastonbury was a ritual invocation, the Grail ritual, designed to recreate the enchantment of ancient times, when the Celtic, Bronze age kingdom at Glastonbury was held under the spell of Arthur and his twelve zodiacal followers. The secrets of ritual magic and the techniques of invocation are unknown, but the archetype of paradise remains, and it can be invoked today, just as surely as in any other period, by the power of human yearning. Any individual who abandons the habits of fear and pride, cultivating in their place love for creation and for the divine spirit within and above it, can achieve the paradisial world-view, thus benefiting his own life and improving the lives of those around him. So begins the invocation of paradise, which is surely the most useful, and perhaps the only effective operation which can be undertaken in these present times. These are times of revelations. Glastonbury still conceals many mysteries, but the process of disclosure has already begun, and the first revelations are precisely those which are most appropriate to our present level of understanding.

Bibliography

Allen, Richard H. , *Star Names and their Meaning*. New York, 1899

Ashe, Geoffrey (1), *King Arthur's Avalon*. London, 1957

Ashe, Geoffrey (2), *Avalonian Quest*.

Ashe, Geoffrey (3), *The Glastonbury Tor Maze*. Glastonbury, 1979

Ashe, Geoffrey (4), (editor) *The Quest for Arthur's Britain*. London, 1968

Berresford Ellis, Peter, *Celtic Inheritance* London, 1985

Bond, Frederick Bligh (1), *An Architectural History of Glastonbury Abbey*. Glastonbury, 1909 (reprinted 1981)

Bond, Frederick Bligh (2), *The Gate of Remembrance*. Oxford, 1918

Bond, Frederick Bligh (3), *The Company of Avalon*. Oxford, 1924

Bond, Frederick Bligh (4), *The Glastonbury Scripts*. Glastonbury, 1925

Bond, Frederick Bligh (5), *The Mystery of Glaston and her Immortal Traditions*. London, 1939

Broadhurst, Paul, and Hamish Miller, *The Sun and the Serpent*. Cornwall, 1989

Bund, J. Willis, *The Celtic Church of Wales*. London, 1987

Burl, Aubrey, *The Stonehenge People*. London, 1989

Carley, James P. (1), 'Melkin the Bard and Esoteric Tradition at Glastonbury Abbey' in *The Downside Review*, 99, 1981

Carley, James P. (2), *Glastonbury Abbey, the Holy House at the Head of the Moors Adventurous*. Woodbridge, 1988

Carley, James P. (3), (editor) *John of Glastonbury's 'Cronica'* (Latin text with notes). Oxford, 1978

Coles, Bryony and John, *Sweet Track to Glastonbury: the Somerset Levels in Prehistory*. London, 1986

Coles, J.M, and B.J. Orne, *Prehistory of the Somerset Levels*. Exeter, 1982

Critchlow, Keith, 'Notes on the Geometry of Stonehenge with Comments on the Ming T'ang,' in *Britain: a Study in Patterns*. London, 1971 (revised edition as *Glastonbury & Britain, A Study in Patterns*, 1990)

Deanesley, Margaret, *The Pre-Conquest Church in England*. London, 1961

Devereux, Paul and Ian Thompson, *The Ley-Hunter's Companion*. London, 1979.

Ditmas, E.M.R. (1), *Traditions and Legends of Glastonbury*. Guernsey, 1979

Ditmas, E.M.R. (2), *Glastonbury Tor: Fact and Legend*. Guernsey, 1981

Dobson, Rev. C.C., *Did Our Lord Visit Britain as They Say in Cornwall and Somerset?* Glastonbury, 1936

Fortune, Dion, *Avalon of the Heart*. London, 1938 (revised edition, 1986)

Geoffrey of Monmouth, *The History of the Kings of Britain*. (1186), translated by Lewis Thorpe. London, 1966

Gibbs, Ray, *The Legendary XII Hides of Glastonbury*. Lampeter, 1988

Goodall, John A. 'The Glastonbury Memorial Plate Reconsidered' in *The Antiquaries Journal*, 66, 1986

Greswell, Rev. William H.P., *Chapters in the Early History of Glastonbury Abbey*. Taunton, 1909

Guichard, Xavier, *Eleusis Alésia*. Paris, 1936 (Trans. C. Rhone, 1985)

Howard-Gordon, Frances, *Glastonbury—Maker of Myths*. Glastonbury, 1982

Kenawell, William W. *The Quest at Glastonbury: a Biographical Study of Frederick Bligh Bond*. New York, 1965

Lewis, Rev. H. A., *Christ in Cornwall and Glastonbury the Holy Land of Britain*. 1939

Lewis, Rev. Lionel Smithett, *St Joseph of Arimathea at Glastonbury or the Apostolic Church of Britain*. Wells, 1922 (enlarged 1937)

Maltwood, K.E., *A Guide to Glastonbury's Temple of the Stars*. London, 1929

Mann, Nick (1), *The Cauldron and the Grail*. Glastonbury, 1985

Mann, Nick (2), *Glastonbury Tor: a Guide to the History and Legends*. Glastonbury, 1986

Michell, John (1), *The View over Atlantis*. London, 1969 (revised as *The New View over Atlantis*, 1983)

Michell, John (2), *City of Revelation*. London, 1972

Michell, John (3), *The Dimensions of Paradise*. London, 1988

Michell, John, and Christine Rhone, *Twelve-Tribe Nations and the Science of Enchanting Landscapes*. London, 1990

Moon, Adrian, *The First Ground of God: a History of the Glastonbury Abbey Estates*. Glastonbury, 1978

Morgan, Rev. R.W., *St Paul in Britain; or the Origin of British as Opposed to Papal Christianity*. London, 1860

Muir, Richard, *Shell Guide to Reading the Celtic Landscapes*. London, 1985

Porter, H.M., *The Celtic Church in Somerset*. Bath, 1971

Rahtz, P. and Hirst, S., *Beckery Chapel, Glastonbury, 1967-68 (report on excavation)*. Glastonbury, 1974

Roberts, Anthony (1), *Sowers of Thunder: Giants in Myth and History*. London, 1978

Roberts, Anthony (2), (editor) *Glastonbury—Ancient Avalon, New Jerusalem*. London, 1976

Robinson, J. Armitage. *Two Glastonbury Legends: King Arthur and St Joseph of Arimathea*. Cambridge, 1926

Scott, John (editor), *The Early History of Glastonbury: An Edition, Translation and Study of William of Malmesbury's 'De Antiquitate...'* Woodbridge, 1981

Snell, F.J., *King Arthur's Country*. London, 1926

Soothill, William E., *The Hall of Light*. London, 1951

Treharne, R. F., *The Glastonbury Legends*. London, 1967

Tudor Pole, Wellesley (editor), *Michael, Prince of Heaven*. London, 1951

Warner, Rev. Richard, *An History of the Abbey of Glaston; and of the Town of Glastonbury*. Bath, 1826

Weston, Jessie L., *From Ritual to Romance*. Cambridge, 1920

William of Malmesbury, *See Scott, J.*

Williams, Hugh, *Christianity in Early Britain*. Oxford, 1912

Williams, Mary, and Janette Jackson (editors), *Glastonbury, A Study in Patterns*. London, 1970 (revised edition as *Glastonbury & Britain, A Study in Patterns*, 1990)

Willis, Rev. R., *The Architectural History of Glastonbury Abbey*. Cambridge, 1866

Index

GOTHIC IMAGE
P U B L I C A T I O N S

Gothic Image Publications is a Glastonbury-based imprint dedicated to publishing books and pamphlets that offer a new and radical approach to our perception of the world in which we live.

As ideas about the nature of life change, we aim to make available those new perspectives which clarify our understanding of ourselves and the Earth we share.

Devas, Fairies and Angels: A Modern Approach
William Bloom   £3.50

Dragons—Their History and Symbolism
Janet Hoult   £4.95

Eclipse of the Sun: An Investigation into Sun & Moon Myths
Janet McCrickard   £9.95

Glastonbury—Maker of Myths
Frances Howard-Gordon   £4.95

The Glastonbury Tor Maze
Geoffrey Ashe   £2.25

The Green Lady and the King of Shadows
A Glastonbury Legend   £4.95

Hargreaves' New Illustrated Bestiary
Joyce Hargreaves   £10.95

Meditation in a Changing World
William Bloom   £6.95

Needles of Stone Revisited
Tom Graves   £6.95

Spiritual Dowsing
Sig Lonegren   £5.50